Advanced Salmon Fishing

R.V. Righyni

Advanced
Salmon Fishing

Macdonald General Books
Macdonald and Jane's · London and Sydney

Published by Macdonald General Books
Macdonald and Jane's Publishing Group Limited
Paulton House
8 Shepherdess Walk, London N1 7LW

ISBN 0 356 04218 9

Printed and bound in Great Britain by
REDWOOD BURN LIMITED
Trowbridge & Esher

Contents

Preface

Our accumulated knowledge of the salmon and the methods of fishing for it can be likened to a jigsaw puzzle.

Some anglers would undoubtedly say that many of the pieces are unavailable and will inevitably remain so: that the picture cannot possibly be completed.

I feel that all the pieces are within reach: the trouble is that some of the important ones are very difficult to identify as such, while many of those that have been recognized share similar shapes with others and can easily be put into the wrong place.

No outright cheating is possible, because one cannot get a preview of the true, finished picture. But fairly-made errors and misfits pressed into place in all good faith at earlier dates may remain undetected as being false. Not only do these mar the parts already assembled, but they complicate still further the problem of the gaps for which it has seemed that no piece could be found.

Before proceeding to areas where there is promise of progress to be made, therefore, it is necessary first to check the validity of those parts of the picture which appear to have been established.

Indeed, no alleviation of the penalty can be expected if one endorses at face value the false placing of pieces by others. Thus, each player must finally take responsibility for his own, ultimate picture.

In presenting my effort with the picture for the reader's judgment, I wish to acknowledge my debt to the authors of many books and to the countless anglers and gillies with whom I have had fascinating and rewarding discussions on all aspects of salmon fishing. I have unexpectedly learned items of great value from anglers of little experience: I have been stimulated to find things out for myself by the views of seasoned anglers with which I could not agree; and I have been helped tremendously by watching other rods at work. Above all, as an angler among anglers, I have enjoyed myself enormously.

I should like to think that this book will give some pleasure in return — if not in the reading, then as an eventual result of the content.

1 Principles

1. Inheritances

The recurrence of fairly regular seasonal patterns in salmon
fishing has encouraged many admirable attempts to formulate rules for the general guidance of anglers. The usefulness
within its well known limits of the advice handed down from
successive periods of relatively quick progress has never been
in dispute; and the most popular fishing procedures practised
today are in very close conformity with concepts that have
not changed more than marginally over the years.

Yet the would-be rules are subject to so many known
interruptions and exceptions that they are of little avail when
help is most needed. Undoubtedly experience may then
suggest the solution without any perplexity, but this conso-
lation is denied to the greater numbers whose careers have
not yet matured.

While there is no wish that the sport should be reduced to
the level of an easily acquired craft – of which there is not
the slightest risk – it is equally undesirable that much
fascinating information should remain only vaguely known.
And it is unfortunate for the angler striving to improve his
standard of performance if the best he can be told is that any
lack of instinctive understanding on his part can only be

remedied by the passing of the years that may bestow upon him the hallowed experience that alone can fill the gap.

Clearly the need is to find some reliable principles through which the problem of the day can be safely narrowed down and the suitable alternative methods of fishing placed in the order of relative value. One imagines, of course, that this has been a prime objective of salmon fishers for generations.

Fairly regular re-examinations of the subject over the years, however, have not succeeded in making very far-reaching progress owing to the obstinacy of the barriers created by the well known anomalies. But if the problem is approached differently by making a study of the anomalies and what could be termed the negative features, the changed perspective gives a new and more acceptable line-up of some of the old ideas. Indeed, it shows that the anomalies are mostly wrongly described as such: that they can be seen to be the results that should be reasonably expected of separate, normal phases of the behaviour of the salmon. And although these phases do not tend to occur for such long periods as those that suit the most popular and productive methods, they rank equally as far as soundly based fishing principles are concerned. But perhaps the main advantage is that they make sense of situations that could otherwise appear to be too baffling to be capable of explanation.

Before an attempt can be made to classify the anomalies, however, it is necessary to establish what can fairly be called an anomaly in the context of the traditional view of normal sport. There must be no confusion between anomalies and purely freak happenings.

The position today is more complicated, but before the appearance of UDN, it was commonly recognized that a salmon suffering from an injury or infirmity was liable to behave most uncharacteristically.

On an altogether hopeless day when numerous experienced rods fishing a variety of well stocked beats could only account for an odd fish or two between them, it was usually found that they bore wounds caused by nets, predators or parasites. If there was no visible injury, an internal inspection probably revealed one of the unpleasant things that can plague a salmon.

Freak catches are not, of course, restricted to bad days and irrespective of whether the healthy fish are responding or not, the take of an infirm fish can often be identified instantly, some of the offers being very spectacular. A typical example can occur when a big spinning lure, after being fished round slowly and close to the bottom in conformity with the policy considered best for the circumstances, is lifted to the surface and retrieved rapidly in preparation for the next cast. A salmon may make a wild charge at a tangent across the top of the water and attack the lure furiously. This cannot be taken as an indication that the well-proved, orthodox method of presentation at that time is wrong and that a fast-moving surface lure has worthwhile merit.

Excessive physical irritation can undoubtedly cause extra-ordinary behaviour, which should be ignored in the context of sound fishing principles for the normal, healthy stocks of salmon. Freak happenings do, however, serve to accentuate what is, in fact, the normal behaviour of the fish that are free from untoward discomfort.

It should be added that there is no evidence to suggest that the incidence of maladjustment of the senses is any greater in the salmon than in other species. On the contrary, it would seem that a handicapped salmon would have far less chance of surviving to full maturity than a non-migratory fish that does not have to adjust to great changes of environment. There are certainly no grounds for making provision in basic fishing policies for any other than completely healthy salmon.

Returning to the question of *genuine anomalies,* these must naturally be viewed against the general run of sport that is considered to be normal. And since the take of a fish can be thought to be anomalous for a variety of very different reasons, it is necessary to deal with the subject by means of a brief survey of an entire season. It so happens also that the seemingly best and most useful of the would-be rules in salmon fishing can be partly examined by the same process.

The ensuing sequence is not as tidy as can be arranged when factors are considered in isolation; also it calls for some patience in awaiting the build-up of interim findings into complete final views. Since the arbitrary narrowing of the contexts of problems has probably been responsible in the past for some of the misconceptions, however, there should be no objection to tackling the increased complexity arising from not yielding to convenience and artificial orderliness.

II. Lure sizes vis-à-vis water temperatures

Historically it has been thought that the temperature of the water governs the size of the artificial lure that should be used; with the speed of the current and the degree of colour in the water as subsidiary influences. Broadly, the dimensions suggested run from about 3½in. for the lowest water temperatures to as small as ¼in. at 60°F and above.

Practical fishing has regularly seemed to confirm that there is a great deal of truth in the idea, despite the glaring anomalies; and no better suggestion having come to light, the idea remains the basic tenet followed today.

The appropriate policy lends itself to division into four well established phases.

Below 42°F – the early season bracket – there is universal agreement that both flies and spinning baits should be about 2¾in. to 3½in. and fished very slowly and close to the bottom.

In what can be termed the transitional period, from 42°F to 48°F, there is not nominally the same amount of unanimity of opinion, but in practice the differences are probably not as great as they are sometimes thought to be. Among fly fishers, some persevere with sunk-line outfits, while others think that the floating-line method can often be the best. But the bracket of fly sizes is much the same in both cases – say 1in. to 2in. – and since the one now keeps his fly considerably further from the bottom and the other tries to get his lure fairly well down from the surface, they both frequently fish at much the same level – roughly the mid-water zone in the medium depth water which is now most favoured. Spinning baits are reduced to around 2in. and fished appreciably higher in the water and faster than earlier in the season.

From 48°F upwards, the orthodox floating-line method is used almost exclusively by fly fishers in all reasonably normal conditions. The lure is fished very much in the surface area, and starting at about 1in. in length, the sizes are steadily and systematically reduced until the water temperature tops the sixty mark. Some scales showing the size recommended for each degree of temperature are observed meticulously by many anglers.

Towards the end of the season when anglers are seeking the true autumn-run salmon, there are again considerable differences of opinion. But this time they amount to more real variations in practice. Some prefer the floating line and lures in accordance with a temperature/size scale whenever conditions seem favourable, while others fish the sunk line and flies that are at least rather large, almost regardless of the temperature of the water and the state of the weather.

Disregarding the anomalies for the moment, this amount of support for the temperature/size idea looks very impressive. But no-one imagines that the artificial lure is of any interest to the salmon as such and it is accepted unreservedly that the illusory image created in the brain of the fish is responsible for any positive interest shown. And at first glance it seems absurd to suggest that the temperature of the water can be involved in a chain of events initiated by an optical illusion.

Attempts have been made to argue on the lines that certain temperatures are associated with certain sizes of natural food during the feeding days at sea and that only the corresponding size of illusion at any temperature is realistic enough to arouse response. In the absence of other ideas, this could be thought to be not untenable, but clearly, any known direct effects of the temperature on the fish must first be investigated.

Being cold-blooded, the salmon acquires its body temperature from the water and in turn, the temperature of the blood affects the rate of metabolism of the fish.

In low temperatures, the fish tends to be very sluggish and quiet. It remains in the steadier, deeper water of the lower reaches and shows no inclination to proceed with its migration upstream to faster, shallower stretches as long as the true winter-type temperatures persist.

Observations going back a great length of time have established that at below 42°F salmon will not ascend very fast, heavy currents where there is a lot of white water, such as that usually to be seen below weirs and other obstructions. The lack of solidarity against which to get leverage when the water is full of small air bubbles makes it very hard work at any temperature for the fish to get sufficient propulsion to leap over obstacles. Nevertheless, once the reading reaches 42°F the salmon show a tendency to make the effort. And after a further slight rise in the temperature, the upstream migrations of the fish cease to be halted by the white water.

When the water temperature reaches the upper fifties, the salmon often give unmistakable proof that they are capable of very great physical exertion when it is needed. And on the purely physical side there can be no doubt that the change in the rate of metabolism makes a large enough difference to be an extremely important factor in the general behaviour of the fish.

The best evidence of what happens to the salmon in the mental sphere as a result of the water temperature is, of course, to be found in analysing what happens and what does not happen in practical fishing.

At very low readings, the large, showy lure must be almost dangled in front of the nose of the fish, which will only move a short distance to make the interception. On the occasions when it is possible to watch the performance, one can see that the salmon closes its mouth on the lure very slowly. But in summer, the fish will rise through several feet of very strong current to meet a tiny fly near to the surface at a point two or three yards ahead of its lie. The spotting of the fly soon enough and the co-ordination required for a successful interception are most significant. The salmon then closes its mouth quite quickly and if it feels any resistance from the line, the fly is spat out instantly.

Thus the known behaviour leaves no doubt that the rate of metabolism has a parallel effect on the physical and mental capabilities of the salmon. The sluggish physical conduct imposed on the fish by low temperatures is accompanied by mental lethargy, while at summer readings the greatly enhanced physical capability is matched by a suitably improved state of mental alertness. This is of fundmental importance because it gives an invaluable guide both to the size of the lure and the way it should be fished.

When it is reflected that a tiny fly at a big distance can cause the same impact as a very large lure at extremely short range owing to a difference in the water temperature, one begins to realize how keenly susceptible the salmon is to the state of its environment. And if one item can have such dramatic influences, it should not be surprising if it is found that other water factors play much more than a minor part in respect of the behaviour of the fish.

A closer look at practical fishing is now needed to reveal the anomalies.

In the early season when the large, slow-moving lures are being used without question and producing satisfactory sport on normal days, only one phenomenon is likely to occur that could be classed as an anomaly. But it is not very common and many anglers who fish regularly during the period have never experienced it personally. When a spate following a spell of wet weather is fining down, the water temperature is usually well up in the higher part of the cold bracket. (Good rainfall automatically means relatively mild overhead conditions and the big volume of water retains its temperature better than when the river is low.) Many of the resident salmon are content with their locations and remain in them, while others may take the opportunity to move upstream a short distance to fresh pools, although there will be no urge as yet for any mass departure from the lower reaches of the river. Such conditions also encourage fresh runs of salmon through the estuary and into the fresh water.

On many beats sport will be good with the normal fishing methods, but most likely with the lure fishing a little faster and a foot or so clear of the bottom. And although it may be noted that some of the fish are on the move upstream, it will probably and correctly be thought that the chances of response from them are negligible compared with the settled fish. In one particular type of water, however, it is not difficult to get offers from travelling fish provided it is a big run, or that the salmon remain in fairly compact schools for the journey. Smooth water with the gliding characteristic — a very evenly paced flow — that extends for a good distance is required for the best results. The same kinds of large and showy lures as for the normal methods are suitable, but they must be fished just beneath the surface and made to cross the tracks of the running salmon as slowly as possible. Some of the takes are very exciting. The fish moves slightly off course to make the interception and its back may break the surface as it is doing so.

In rougher, irregular currents, it is exceedingly difficult to induce a salmon to make the most minor diversion from the course it is taking along the grain of the flow; and as the chance that the lure will appear just at the right moment directly in front of a fish is so slight, that class of water is not really worth fishing for runners.

Salmon remain very near the surface when travelling, of course, and, in effect, the actual presentation of the lure to them when they do take is at as close quarters as when fishing for settled residents on the bottom. As the lures are also no different, the only feature that could appear to be anomalous is that ordinarily the large lure is only expected to be effective on or near the bottom, but in this case it is successful near the surface.

In terms of the behaviour of the salmon, therefore, the take of the running fish near the surface can be accepted as a perfectly natural phase that should not cause any doubt or confusion.

During the transitional period – 42°F to 48°F – the variety of ways in which salmon are caught that are in keeping with the popular concepts is so great that it is not easy to pick out the occurrences that could be regarded as abnormal. The thoughtful beginner, however, is quick to comment on the tendency of spinning baits to be appreciably larger than the flies used at the same time, which appears odd to him. Seasoned anglers see nothing remarkable in this and thus show the general acceptance of the belief that the speed at which a lure is fished has a significant bearing on the size that can effectively create a suitable illusion. In the cold water conditions, all lures usually having been fished at much the same speed, there was virtually no difference in the lengths of the flies and spinners, but now, as a result of regular popular practice and success, this kind of quali-fication in respect of the size of the lure emerges quite convincingly.

Probably the only seemingly outright anomaly that may be noticed during this period is that anglers fishing with conventional wet-fly tackle for brown trout occasionally hook a salmon. Such artificials as the Orange Partridge and March Brown dressed on hooks as small as no. 14 have, in the aggregate, undoubtedly attracted response from too great a number of salmon for it to be ignored. It may also be discovered that two salmon flies of appreciable difference in size that hooked salmon at approximately the same time were being fished at much the same speed and depth in the same class of water.

Evidence of that kind is considered by some anglers to be absolute proof of the fallibility of the temperature/size rule. Before attempting to reach any final conclusion in that regard, however, it is necessary to look a little further into the seasonal changes.

Many more beats on the earliest of the rivers and on an increasing number of other rivers begin to offer prospects of good sport when the higher bracket of water temperatures is reached – 48°F upwards – and the floating-line method becomes regularly effective. Now a vastly greater number of anglers are likely to be fishing on any one day and the evidence is much more broadly based.

Methodically minded anglers adhere conscientiously to some form of size rule and although there is a marked similarity in the bulk of the choices made for any particular situation, there is often a big difference between the two extremes that may account for fish. The result is that almost side by side, Low Water nos 5 and 7 may both attract offers. To the eye of the experienced salmon fisher this difference is tremendous, but seemingly the fish do not mind.

After a further rise in the water temperature has brought a corresponding all round reduction in sizes, there appears to be greater agreement generally. With the water at 60°F or more and no colour or wind to suggest any reason to take liberties, few anglers would think of trying anything bigger than a Low Water no. 8 and most would probably have more confidence in a no. 9. Indeed, they would not criticise a no. 10 excepting to say that there is a tendency to lose too many fish with such a small iron. At this stage, then, it would appear that faith in the old temperature/size rule is beginning to grow again. At the same time, it may suddenly become subject to fresh doubt that is considered by some anglers to be the fatal blow.

In a big, clear water following a good spate, or on a spring-fed river or one draining a large area of still water, one angler may have some success with a Low Water no. 8, while not far away another rod gets response to a 2in. tube-fly fished on a sinking line. This is, of course, one of the classic cases quoted by anglers when disputing the old size rule. But examination of the position is almost certain to show some not unfamiliar features. Firstly, the productive water for the big fly will probably prove to be a fairly long, smooth glide, although the surface may be rippled at the time by some breeze. Secondly the angler will throw a long line at 45° or more downstream and immediately start recovering by long, rather fast draws by the left hand. Now imagine what happens, particularly in regard to the behaviour of the fly. The speed of the flow together with the speed of re-covery ensures that the heavy line does not sink much, but remains just slightly below the surface. And for the same reasons—the effect of the flow on the shortening line—the fly crosses the river practically at right-angles to the flow, only a little below the surface, and not nearly as quickly as the rate of recovery would suggest. Indeed, the fly covers a shorter distance in the time than it would do if the line were allowed to swing round without being shortened during the process. Hence, the fly moves suitably to interest running fish, and it would be very difficult, if not impossible, to achieve the same result with a floating line. And it is true to say that this sunk line/big fly method is very effective in the right place with fresh-run summer salmon before they become settled.

Once again, the apparent anomaly has no meaning that should be allowed to cause doubt or indecision.

Another example is rather similar, but is explained differently. As the level drops on some of the smaller rivers, the streams and runs become too shallow to give adequate cover during the daytime and the salmon collect in the larger, deeper, almost still pools. When a good breeze gets up, local anglers will recommend that one should mount a 1½in. fly, make a long cast into the wind, and recover by long, fairly fast draws. Any surprise expressed when this method succeeds, however, does not seem to take account of the fact that it would not be thought at all extraordinary if a small spinner were to take a fish or two. And as far as the salmon are concerned, there cannot be much difference between the two images. Such methods with the fly – *stripping,* and the rather similar *backing-up* – cannot be regarded, therefore, as being at all anomalous.

The cooling of the water as autumn approaches sees a certain amount of confirmation for the temperature/size rule but moodily-tempered red fish are now in the majority and not much attention is paid to such salmon. The real remaining interest of the season is the arrival of the autumn-run fish, straight from the sea.

As mentioned earlier, the differences of opinion among anglers are now very real. Conventional floating-line fishing can certainly be successful when overhead conditions are pleasant, but it is probably true to say that more fish are taken on the sunk line. The crucial point, however, is that the largest early season flies will take autumn-run fish at all sorts of depths when the water temperature is well above the bracket in which they are used for the springers. The decision, therefore, must undoubtedly be that the temperature/size rule simply does not apply to autumn-run salmon.

This really does seem to be a genuine anomaly at this juncture, but there is one interesting clue that calls for investigation before accepting such a finding. Anglers who are very familiar with autumn-run salmon make an almost invariable drill of keeping the big fly moving by a series of long draws of line after it has fished round through the faster flow. And many will say that they get more offers during this final manoeuvre than when the fly is behaving in the more conventional way. Naturally, this action results in the lure rising nearer to the surface at a steep incline with each successive draw.

Unfortunately an entirely different feature of the behaviour of the salmon must be considered in the effort to resolve this latest problem. The delay caused in sorting out the findings made so far is regrettable but essential.

III. Why salmon take
Few anglers can deny having participated keenly in the ever popular debate on the motives that prompt the salmon to respond to a lure.

The alternatives usually discussed, however, could rarely be said to exhaust the possible scope; and the context in which they are viewed is often too narrow for any answer to appear very much more sound than another. Also there is a tendency to argue on the premise that there is a single solution, and that may be false.

Fortunately the scientists have settled the first, fundamental question. They state that the salmon does not feed in fresh water: that even the old belief of anglers that the fish chews a worm to suck out the juices is definitely untrue.

In language that the layman can readily understand, the books explain how numerous physical changes take place — amounting in some cases to alterations in the function of some of the organs — to accommodate the salmon to life in the freshwater habitat, which is so very different chemically from the sea.

Perhaps the salmon is not prevented from performing the physical act of swallowing temporarily some small item, and this may be misleading; but the angler must accept that there is simply no room for argument against the scientific evidence that the mature fish does not feed in fresh water.

Knowing that the salmon's accumulated store of energy is adequate for its rigorous spawning visit to the river and any question of an appetite for food being dispelled, the popular list of possibilities to be considered comprises reflex action as a hangover from the feeding habits at sea; curiosity; and aggressive behaviour for a variety of different reasons. It is common among many species of animals — presumably including the salmon — to attack and destroy maimed specimens of their own and other species, which is no doubt part of nature's general scheme to ensure a healthy environment. Aggressive behaviour is also shown towards other species that may deprive the young of food, or threaten the lives of the progeny more directly.

Yet the general conduct of the salmon in returning to the river and ultimately arriving at the breeding grounds on time appears to be largely a matter of involuntary response to various compelling circumstances. Aggressiveness could, of course, arise involuntarily out of the need for self preservation, but also it could possibly be voluntary. The basic question, therefore, is whether the salmon is capable in any way of genuinely voluntary action, and if so, the extent to which such action is involved. In this respect, the results of some interesting old experiments and certain less attractive, more recent events are very helpful.

From time to time anglers have found good lies for salmon where they could lower a worm or a prawn into the water, hold it in position on the bottom in front of a fish, and observe everything in detail while they waited for something to happen. Sometimes either one of the baits was taken promptly. Occasionally the prawn scared the fish away permanently. The worm would sometimes cause the salmon to move off for a short time, but invariably it eventually returned to its lie. And almost without exception the worm, and the prawn if the fish remained in position, would be taken sooner or later. Very often there would be no activity for quite a few minutes — which is a very long time in these circumstances — but it was very rare that the bait was not taken within a quarter of an hour. The anglers concerned were satisfied from their copious experience that their experiments had covered the kinds of conditions both when the salmon in general would have been in a taking mood, and when they would not have been interested at all in artificial lures, fished normally, of course.

Recently there have been numerous occurrences showing support for this suggestion that a salmon will take a worm when it is definitely disinterested from the normal fishing point of view. When there have been some obviously diseased fish among a good stock of apparently healthy salmon and conditions have seemed excellent for good sport to be expected, very skilful anglers with both fly and spinner have often been unable to get an offer of any sort. Then, in desperation, one of them has decided to try a worm. Eventually there would be extensive indications of interference with the bait, but nothing would come of it. This would sometimes happen again and again, and ultimately a fish would be successfully hooked and landed.

The broad inference was that the disease seemed to have had an adverse effect on the disposition of the salmon generally, and that perhaps many of the apparently healthy fish were slightly infected. But combined with the discoveries made before the appearance of UDN, this taking of a worm in circumstances that were undoubtedly very dispiriting to the salmon suggests a motive which does not seem to have been suspected previously. Probably arising basically from irritation, the intention of the fish may have been nothing more than it appeared to be — simply to pick up the worm, move away and drop it again in a position well clear, and then return to the lie: in other words, a straightforward *house-cleaning* operation without belligerent or aggressive intent, but definitely suggesting voluntary action.

If such a finding has the substance that one may believe it to have, it would indicate that the salmon is, indeed, not invulnerable to induced responsive action. And in view of this, it would be interesting to have a means of knowing whether any aggressiveness shown by a fish was the result of fear or pure belligerence of spirit, as this would indicate the tactics to adopt. And there is some fairly clear evidence in this respect.

It is not uncommon for salmon to be hooked in the fleshy part of the tail when anglers are fishing perfectly legitimately and correctly in the downstream and across method with large lures. Also there are knocks which produce nothing and seem to be too quick and heavy for proper takes. And on rather rare occasions, a salmon is seen to come quickly upstream and give the lure a mighty crack with the tail as it passes. Now consider one of the habits of the trout. It swims through a shoal of minnows thrashing its tail violently from side to side, and then returns to collect the casualties. Clearly the most offensive weapon possessed by the members of the salmon family is the tail. And since the salmon loses its sea-feeding teeth before entering the fresh water, the most lethal attack it can make is undoubtedly with the tail; and this is probably the explanation of the foul hookings. Supposing this deduction to be correct, it means, of course, that no deed performed with the jaws or mouth can be assumed to be an act of maximum aggression; if, in fact, the motive is even as aggressive as the action suggests.

With the clue to the state of mind of the salmon in accordance with the temperature of the water, however, and with experience of the physical performance of the fish when taking a lure at the different periods of the season, it is now possible to formulate a general idea of the motives involved on lines that are not by any means entirely abstract.

In the very cold water early in the season, many of the takes feel to be very gentle — nothing more than the lure simply being stopped. Sometimes one gets the impression of a very solid pull, but free from any sense of violence or agitation; this is probably due to the pressure of the water on the line following a take that is no less gentle than the one that feels to be so. At temperatures in the higher part of the very cold bracket, a fish may be seen to be following the spinner as it approaches the side and then take as it turns to go back to its lie. The performance does not appear to be very aggressive, but it is certainly more so than the very gentle take.

On the whole it seems that at this time of the year, involuntary reflex action is more in evidence than anything suggesting much aggressiveness. And this is in keeping with both the fact that the time which has elapsed since the fish were at sea is short, and the currently *dreamy* state of their mentality.

Evidence of an aggressive motive – for whatever specific reason – is to be seen during the transitional period. This, however, remains very much a feature of spinning when the lure is moving through the water comparatively quickly. Rises to the fly put one more in mind of the collecting of food than an attack on some creature with the primary objective of killing it.

In the summer temperature bracket, rises to the fly are often beautifully graceful. The co-ordination is perfect with the opening and closing of the mouth seemingly not a fraction more than is necessary, and certainly without a vestige of anger or irritability. One could imagine, however, that the little flip of the tail as the turn is made to go down again has an element of swank about it. Indeed, the whole incident has the appearance of showing off.

Success with spinning at the higher water temperatures up to about the end of July requires very much more effort than at the lower temperatures and rarely gives consistently good results unless there is a fair amount of help in the way of colour in the water or a good stiff breeze.

All this tends to show that when the mental state of the salmon is at its potentially most alert stage, the influences which cause the type of response thought to be involuntary reflex action are not weakened, whereas the kind of reaction which appears to involve some aggressiveness is more difficult to induce.

Yet at this time when the water is relatively warm and quite clear, if an angler goes to a well stocked pool which has been left undisturbed that day, and makes a long cast with a large wobbling spoon — the size used in the early season — he will probably arouse some interest as he retrieves the lure very rapidly. A salmon may just make a slight move towards the spoon and quickly shy away, or perhaps follow it for some distance. Occasionally the fish may give the bait a knock, or even take it and get hooked. The first cast, however, is the only one likely to produce any pronounced reaction and certainly after two or three trips made by the spoon, the salmon will ignore it entirely.

One can reasonably deduce from this that although the large, fast-moving lure retains its power to create an illusion capable of arousing interest that appears to be aggressive, motives of such a nature are not now strong enough to dominate the fish after the novelty effect has been lost. And since the small spinner skillfully used will sometimes produce some sport, but not nearly as much as can be enjoyed with the small subsurface fly, the acceptable finding is that up to about the end of July, mild-tempered reflex action appears to be a much more important influence than anything to do with aggressiveness.

It will be appreciated, of course, that there has been no attempt to suggest that aggression is an essential part of the response to fast-moving spinning lures. The point requiring to be established is simply that aggressiveness is apparently not a very important feature of the behaviour of salmon up to the end of July.

From August onwards, however, when most of the salmon are coloured or inclining that way, there is a marked increase in the tendency of the fish to show an aggressive attitude. With both fly and spinner, many of the offers look more like belligerent attacks than involuntary impulses simply to intercept and take hold of a lure. Male fish are frequently hooked in the top of the kype or the cavity at the front of the upper jaw: this gives the impression that the intention is to nip the lure and not simply to gather it in the mouth.

When the autumn salmon fresh from the sea make their appearance there is very little time to elapse before the males will be standing guard over the completed redds after the females have departed for restful lies. And if there is a time when the fish are aggressively minded towards anything which may threaten the progeny, it must surely be during this final phase of the season when the autumn-run salmon give the angler a brief chance for some extraordinarily good sport.

The rather special tactics that produce good catches on lures that are often very large in relation to the water temperature support this suggestion. And since evidence of a change in the disposition of the salmon starts to be detectable in August, after which it appears to progress at an accelerating rate, it seems very probable that the motive of the autumn-run fish is predominantly one of aggression, if not entirely so.

In the circumstances it will no doubt be agreed that the behaviour of the autumn-run salmon should be seen as a separate phase in its own right, and not something to be regarded as anomalous.

Much more remains to be considered before all the points discussed can be applied usefully, but the outline of the findings concerning lure sizes can now be formulated.

IV. Amended rules for lure sizes
The word rule is used for convenience without any dogmatic intention. Individuals will naturally make their own assessments. If, however, the findings portray the reader's personal interpretation of the evidence of the behaviour of the salmon which has been mentioned so far, he will not be very concerned about the formality of the word.

It must also be said that not too fine a point should be made of the specific lengths to be mentioned, which cannot pretend to be more than average estimates.

The principal finding is that the question of lure sizes breaks down into three different phases, each requiring its own separate treatment.

1. Salmon settled in pools from the beginning of the season until about the end of July.

The water temperature gives a most useful guide to the size of lure that is likely to create a suitable illusion according to the speed at which it is fished. In principle, the old temperature/size rule is confirmed, excepting that the size indicated should be taken to be the *largest* size to be used. There is no problem in this respect when the water temperature is in the early season bracket – up to $42^{\circ}F$. But during the transitional period and the floating line season, smaller sizes than indicated by the temperature can undoubtedly succeed in making an effective illusion. (It will be seen later, however, that the size indicated by the temperature is the most reliable in several respects.)

The popularly-used sizes for the water temperatures in the early season and the transitional period have already been stated. The scale applicable to the floating-line season – which was the most suspect owing to the previously confusing successes of both smaller and very much larger sizes than indicated – can now command much confidence. A useful version of the scale is:

Water Temperature $^{\circ}F$	Low Water Hook Size No.
48 – 49	4
50 – 51	5
52 – 53	6
54 – 55	7
56 – 57	8
58 – 59	9
60 and over	10

There is no intention, of course, that the scale should be observed too rigidly. Naturally, the speed of the flow may call for some adjustment, as may the tactics employed by the individual. But as a reliable starting-off point, the scale usually proves to be remarkably successful.

Subsidiary findings for this phase are as follow.

(a) Response to slow-moving lures appears to be predominantly of the involuntary reflex action type, and therefore is probably restricted to definite taking times in all cases when the fish is required to rise to make an interception.

(b) In the low-temperature bracket, slow-moving lures fished at eye level which may threaten to bump the salmon on the nose may be taken although the fish is not in an alert, responsive mood.

(c) The aggressive motive cannot be ruled out when relatively fast-moving lures are taken. This may mean that response of that sort can be induced when conditions fall somewhat short of the requirements to produce a willing taking mood. Hence, spinning may sometimes have some success when conventional floating-line and midwater fly-fishing fail to produce any response.

2. Running salmon while actually travelling, should be treated as a separate problem at all times. The lures should always be large — both flies and spinners — and fished slowly just beneath the surface. At water temperatures below 48°F and also at higher temperatures if the water is at all coloured, around 3½in. is the most suitable size. When the water is clear and above 48°F, it may be better to reduce the size to as small as 2in. according to the speed of the flow and the state of the light.

3. From August onwards the temperature/size rule diminishes in effectiveness in a way thought to be proportionate to the degree to which the aggressive motive becomes dominant.

When the autumn-run salmon enter the rivers, the rule can be considered to be almost entirely inoperative. Large lures which may induce aggressive response are generally the most effective, irrespective of the water temperature; and may take fish at all levels, from very near the bottom to just beneath the surface.

The final confirmation of the temperature/size rule cannot be seen, however, until the question of patterns has been considered, because there is much evidence to show that these two features of the lure are closely interactive.

V. The colour of the lure

It was thought a long time ago that colour in its own right could be attractive to the salmon and that they could associate colour with some kinds of natural food. Since those days, fortunately, there has been enough evidence produced in the form of practical fishing results to establish very sound principles covering certain parts of the season and to give very good pointers for other times.

There is no longer any need for anglers to tease themselves with attempts to produce images for the salmon representing unknown or assumed items of food. It could be thought that the work done on those lines originally is what eventually led up to the patterns that are now known to be extremely suitable in certain conditions. But today, when much more is known about this subject of the salmon's natural food at sea, there is no inducement to use the information in an attempt to *improve* the lures that have done well for many years. Indeed, some of the currently available spinners that look very much like some of the small fish that the salmon are known to eat are not at all popular.

Clearly anglers of some experience today accept that the illusion which evokes the response of the non-feeding salmon depends more on the optical factors at the time than on any possibility of a faithful representation of food having been fortuitously established.

Unfortunately the range of patterns of flies and spinning baits that is available on the market grossly exaggerates the requirements and can be confusing: it should be regarded as the needless hangover from the days when the process of trial and error was in its early stages.

The easiest approach to the problem as currently seen is to look first at the most consistently successful small groups of patterns and evaluate the images created in the circumstances in which they prove suitable.

At the beginning of the season, experienced anglers know just what they will need — no second thought requires to be given to the selection. The first line of artificials comprises the large Yellow Belly Devon Minnow in wood or plastic and the three inch bucktail flies, predominantly yellow but including small strips of red, orange, brown or black. The second string comprises the Brown and Gold, or Black and Gold Devon and bucktail fly in lemon with black strips. The third string comprises 3½in. wobbling spoons in all-silver, all-gold, and black and gold; and similar lures. (The Golden Sprat — still a highly popular lure — has not been forgotten, but its semi-natural status makes it unsuitable for consideration in this particular context.)

First take an average sort of day in January or February with a grey sky and very little sunshine. The salmon will be lying quietly in deep water — anything from about six or eight feet to twenty or more. The big yellow artificial is fished slowly across the flow and the fish moves forward to intercept it at a point about a yard or so in front of its nose.

In order to visualise the type of image seen by the salmon, it must first be remembered that at this time of the year, the light at its strongest is relatively weak, and beneath a lot of dark cloud it is very poor. Then, by the time it has penetrated to the bed of the river, a further big loss of strength has taken place. The salmon's view of anything ahead of it at a low angle of sight depends, of course, on reflected light. The diffused light at this depth produces an almost negligible amount of reflection and consequently the general background in the horizontal plane is very dull and practically colourless. The yellow lure reflects a better than average proportion of the light that reaches it and thus results in a palish image seen against a dark background. But it is indeterminate in both shape and colour. In the case of the bucktail fly, the hairs are mobile in the water and the strips of darker colour also help in breaking up any too rigid outline or unnatural uniformity of colour. The slow spin and the variation in colour from a creamy yellow to a dark olive do the same thing for the Yellow Belly Devon. Thus the illusory power of the lure is created by a number of contributory factors.

Needless to say, an object coloured exactly the same as the background would be extremely difficult to detect, while a solid black object against a white background would be seen too clearly in its true form and tone to have any worthwhile illusory power. With these points in mind and recognizing the proven success of the yellow lure, it is clear that the principle involved is that the salmon should see the lure without too much difficulty, but not well enough for its illusory power to be destroyed.

The darker toned of the early season lures are for the brighter days when the lighter colours may be thought to be reflecting too much light and therefore may be seen too determinately. And other patterns in the small selection mentioned give the angler full scope to produce an image with a suitable impact on the fish in any of the circumstances he is likely to meet, including coloured water, when the bright silvers and golds may be required.

While on this topic, however, it should be mentioned that when fishing unobstructed pools in a clear water, the popular preference is that any gold or silver on such lures as the Black and Gold Devon should be of the duller type produced with paint. But for fish in lies where their forward view may be

Above top: The Spey at Grantown seen from the road bridge. In this shallow rapid the extent of the surface exposure proportionate to the volume causes the water to react quickly to the state of the atmosphere.

Above: The Spey at Craigellachie seen from the old road bridge before the erection of the new one. A fine example of a glide: excellent at times for sea trout but seldom worth a cast for salmon.

Above top: The River Awe at Bonawe. Excellent water for the floating line in summer.

Above : The Aberdeenshire Dee at Dinnet. Classic fly water for salmon.

badly restricted owing to weeds and other obstructions, the
metallic silvers and golds that are capable of a bigger impact
are more popular.

Going now to the other extreme of those days in summer
when the small subsurface fly proves to be the most effective
lure, tiny Stoat's Tails regularly account for a lot of fish in
bright, sunny conditions. Viewing the fly against the sky, the
salmon will naturally see only the silhouette. A clearly-seen
stationary silhouette would be useless, of course, but the
movement of the fly plus the tendency of the fish to be
dazzled by strong light evidently result in a sufficiently
indeterminate image for it to be effectively illusory.

These examples demonstrate that the practical way to
approach the problem is to assess the nature of the
background, then judge the colouring of the lure that will
produce an image which will be seen well enough, but not
too clearly for it to create a suitable illusion.

In order to facilitate this procedure, all lures, particularly
subsurface flies, can be classified into categories according to
the density of the image they produce. My own system – I
regret that my effort to remain impersonal in the interests of
objectivity must be relaxed occasionally – is as follows.

VI. Classification of patterns
1. The Silhouette
When it is judged that only the silhouette of the fly can be
seen by the fish in dazzling conditions, a light-toned pattern
may not produce a sufficiently dense image to make the
necessary impact quickly enough, especially in fast water.
The all-black, or predominantly black dressings are the
obvious choice. The Stoat's Tail and Blue Charm are popular
examples of this category.

Silhouette patterns also seem to be the most suitable for
the dusk period and night fishing when the sky is very
overcast. Then the light is too poor for the reflection of
colour generally and everything takes on a very dull grey

appearance. Images that are less dense than black assume a tone very similar to the background and are very difficult to see, particularly against the least dark area, the sky, which is the background for the fish. The black fly makes the best contrast and, therefore, the biggest impact.

2. The Translucent Illusion

Very strong light does not always create a dazzling background for the fish. Particularly in the mornings and evenings, the angle of sight to the fly may result in a very clear image without dazzle. Then a darkish-looking fly may have no power of illusion, while a very light-toned dressing, seen largely by means of transmitted light, would appear less determinate in both shade and form, thus making it more deceptive.

The old saying about bright flies for bright days is confirmation of this view.

The number of very suitable dressings for inclusion in this group is rather small, but any angler who ties some of his own flies will have no difficulty in creating one or two effective patterns. And as with the other groups, there is no need to have many alternatives in the same class. In orthodox patterns, Yellow Torrish, Silver Grey and Silver Blue are popular for this purpose.

3. The Normal Image

This group covers flies composed largely of mixed, medium-toned colours that depend on reflected light to create an image that is neither too glaring nor too nondescript.

When the light is either too poor to impair the vision of the salmon with dazzle, or when it is moderated by some slight colour in the water, the background is not bright, yet not without colour. Then the medium-toned fly is neither too easy nor too difficult to see for its illusory power to be ineffective.

The group includes the Logie, which has a great reputation

for conditions of this kind. Kate and the March Brown (the salmon dressing, of course) are other suitable patterns.

4. The Flashing Illusion

As the name implies, the silver-bodied flies with some very bright or dense colour form this category. Their particular use is in very confined spaces where the fly cannot be fished round properly, such as small, deep, rocky pools in gorges. The salmon can only be given a quick glimpse of the lure as it is made to traverse the taking zone quickly and the impact must be good enough to get instant response. Examples include the Mar Lodge and Silver Doctor.

5. Normal Image/Silhouette (subsidiary category)

With rather more colour in the water than is suitable for the Normal Image, a rather denser image is required to make sufficient impact. This compromise category of black-bodied flies with a good mixture of strong colours in the rest of the dressing is the popular choice. The best example is the Thunder & Lightning. Jock Scott and Hairy Mary would, of course, also be included.

6. Translucent Illusion/Normal Image (subsidiary category)

This compromise with slightly denser colouring than the very pale dressings of the true bright-weather fly is required when it is thought that slightly more impact is needed. In very shallow lies, where the angle of sight is exceptionally low, or in fast, broken water, the very pale image may not be seen soon enough. Lemon Grey is perhaps the best example.

In effect, this division of all patterns of flies into six groups is a contention that all practical requirements can be covered adequately by six basic patterns. A re-examination of the categories will show that it would be making very fine differences if a further class were inserted. Indeed, a more valid criticism would probably be that the six could be reduced to four without much sacrifice, i.e. drop the two compromise categories.

It is well known that many very accomplished anglers consider it unnecessary to use more than just a few patterns. But it need hardly be mentioned that this does not mean to say that they consider it unnecessary to have a full enough selection to suit all the different requirements. And since this can be done quite fully with the six mentioned, and tolerably well on most occasions with four patterns, the problem is clearly one that is infinitely more simple than is suggested by the average fly box.

The principles involved in selecting the patterns of spinning lures are, of course, no different from those already mentioned. The normally bigger size of the spinner tends to compensate for the fact that it moves faster — naturally this excludes the early season — and therefore there is no great need for deeper colour density than in the corresponding fly. At the same time, however, spinning is often resorted to when the current is considered to be on the fast side for fly, and in that case, a rather denser image will sometimes be favoured.

Returning to the question of flies, the finding in relation to the Water Temperature/Lure Size problem that smaller sizes than the one indicated may be successful at any one time is, of course, the cause of possible confusion, and the colour is very much involved.

Small black flies have been responsible for many misconceptions. Some years ago very small Stoat's Tail tube-flies became very popular in certain areas. Compared with flies dressed on Low Water hooks, the tube-flies were very cheap, and having proved their worth, it was not surprising that they became very extensively used. On a bright sunny day in a clear water they were, of course, an excellent choice for fishing slightly beneath the surface for small summer salmon and grilse. In some areas the stage was reached when it became quite a novelty to see any local rod using a different pattern.

This success in the warm weather subsequently led to the small Stoat's Tail being tried much earlier in the season if any difficulty arose in finding a suitable pattern to interest the fish, as it seemed. Not surprisingly, the experiments were not without success.

It was nothing new, of course, to catch fish on smaller flies than conventional ideas suggested. Indeed, it was in line with popular drill to try reductions in size if the salmon proved difficult. When an angler judged that, say, a Low Water no. 6 Logie was right to start with and there was no response after a reasonable spell of fishing, it was standard practice to change to a no. 7, and then perhaps to a no. 8. Sport often came after such alterations had been made, whether or not it was the reduction in size or a sudden change in the mood of the fish that had made a welcome difference.

When notes were exchanged at the end of the day, it was probably found that a variety of patterns of flies in sizes appreciably smaller than suggested by the old rule had all accounted for salmon. This was interpreted by many anglers to mean that it was really the size that mattered, not the pattern, but also that there was no reliable formula for establishing the right size: that trial and error alone could provide the answer.

Although the Stoat's Tail's success had largely been restricted to relatively small sizes on the day, it was held to support the view that size only is important. The argument was that the all-black fly proved either that the salmon is indifferent to colour, or that irrespective of the pattern, it sees only the silhouette when the fly is near the surface. The extension of this was that since several sizes can take fish in the same circumstances, there cannot be any rational order governed by temperature or other factors. Hence the final inference was that the fickle whim of the fish at any one time is the deciding factor in relation to the size of the fly.

As opposed to that kind of experience and thinking, of course, anglers over the years have conducted well organized experiments, supported by careful observation by assistants, concerning the reactions of salmon in their lies. They have proved to their entire satisfaction that a change of pattern without any reduction in size can deceive a salmon that has previously shown abortive interest only. A salmon may make a slight lift from its lie as if to rise and intercept a no. 8 Blue Charm or some other black-bodied fly, only to drop back again without making a close approach. The observer reports the occurrence and after it has been repeated once or twice, the angler substitutes a less densely-toned pattern, say a no. 8 Logie, and then the salmon rises all the way and takes boldly.

Evidence of this nature is much too valuable to be ignored, or discounted on the grounds of less revealing occurrences, and the acceptance of some principle in this respect is important for more than one reason. It will be agreed readily that one does not wish to be getting offers to smaller sizes than necessary because the hook-holds will probably be less reliable. Also, if the fish are willing to take a larger size, whether of the same pattern or a different one, the smaller fly may not always be seen as easily owing to the tricks of the current on the light and the irregularities of the background to the image.

What is perhaps even more serious, however, is that a concise and soundly mastered system helps to remove the element of guesswork. The inexperienced angler is often at a loss to know whether the lack of sport is due to having chosen the wrong method for the occasion; to having failed to discover the right size and pattern of lure; or, on the other hand, if it is because the fish are simply not in a taking mood.

Growing experience and knowledge should make this kind of dilemma less frequent. But the surest way to guard against frequent repetitions of multi-dimensional problems is to acquire sufficient confidence in one's understanding of the principles governing the selection of the pattern of the lure. Clearly if one can accept that basically there are only six patterns from which to choose, the area of doubt is vastly reduced. So much so, in fact, that the problem becomes very much less of a worry than that apparently suffered by those who relegate it to the level of being a matter of indifference.

Patterns of lures will be mentioned again in the chapters on practical fishing, when other features not yet considered will be examined.

VII. Suitability of conditions for fishing (The Oxygen Theory)

The habit of keeping fishing diaries is old and widespread. Individuals note a certain number of details covering the method of fishing, the lure; and the weather and water factors prevailing at the time of each offer, whether or not the fish was hooked and successfully landed. Air temperature, barometric pressure, the relative humidity of the atmosphere, cloud and/or sunshine, the water level and its temperature and colour, all feature in one or another of the records.

Such painstaking efforts show that anglers have long believed that taking times are probably promoted by certain combinations of a variety of influences, and not by one single factor. Their careful attention to the problem has revealed a fairly reliable pattern of seasonal tendencies; and a strong pointer suggesting that some of the unseen factors, such as the atmospheric pressure, play as important a part as the more obvious items. Furthermore, studies of this sort have enabled many anglers to become suitably capable of judging fishing prospects on the day even though they may have made no claim to have solved the problem of the relative values of many factors.

Briefly the pattern which emerges is that, starting at the very low water temperatures, sport is mainly confined to a very few hours in the middle of the day. As the water becomes warmer, the duration of the good period is extended. Eventually a gap in the sport appears in the middle of the day, and this tends to grow as the weather becomes more summerlike. As autumn approaches, the quiet period narrows and eventually disappears. By the time that the autumn-run salmon begin to arrive, sport may be had at almost any hour on a good day.

Additionally there is the overall feature that the dusk period, or the approach to it, often produces good sport irrespective of the time of the year.

At this point it is interesting to note that on this basis of broad averages, the taking times of salmon tend to coincide with the hatches of water-bred flies such as the Large Spring Olive and March Brown. And the experienced trout fisher who can make reliable assessments of the way the weather will affect his sport has no difficulty in this respect when he decides to extend his interest to the salmon.

From a practical fishing point of view, it is highly satisfactory to have confidence in one's judgment as to when to persevere and when a rest can be taken at the least probable cost, yet not to have resolved the problem beyond the stage of generalities. This valuable skill acquired without recourse to the detailed study of the effects of the weather and water factors, however, inevitably involves rather lengthy experience.

No doubt it will be agreed that most individuals who are naturally drawn to angling have an aptitude to understand weather. And armed with further information, which may result in a closer approach to the truth behind taking times, such anglers would probably be able to profit far more quickly and extensively from their earliest experience onwards, thus shortening the overall time required to feel perfectly at home on the river in all reasonably interesting circumstances.

The first step necessary is to widen the context in which the problem is considered. And to be on the safe side, it is best to start right at the beginning.

During its non-feeding visit to the river for spawning, the life of the salmon shows interesting similarities with that of an animal in hibernation. At any one time, its metabolism is relatively very constant throughout the twentyfour hours, and is geared down to suit the need to conserve energy.

Unlike animals engaged in feeding and digesting food regularly, whose supply of energy is on a put and take basis, the good health of the salmon does not depend on a strikingly obvious pattern of periods of exercise, relaxation, rest and sleep.

On the other hand, the salmon cannot descend to the level of the deep, unbroken sleep of the fully hibernated animal, owing to the instability of its environment and the requirement to make the remainder of the journey to the spawning areas. At any moment the fish must be prepared to move away from danger, or seek shelter from very fast currents when the river rises. And although the periodic running operations are probably achieved with far less expenditure of energy than may be imagined, they undoubtedly demand a higher degree of physical and mental alertness than when the fish is resident in a lie.

Only a fraction of the time spent in the river by early-run salmon, of course, is occupied in upstream travel. At the very least they remain in some lies for days on end. And then, apart from the precautions mentioned, they have virtually nothing to do but wait. In the circumstances, it seems reasonable to say that although their senses do not assume an inoperative state, the fish do not remain mentally fully awake the whole of the time. If it is accepted that nature is fundamentally considerate to all creatures, the long periods of apparently complete inactivity must amount to oblivion. It seems, however, that this must not be allowed to continue indefinitely. In low water temperatures, very short spells of slightly increased consciousness appear to be adequate, but at higher readings, both the extent and the duration of the increase in mental and physical alertness required of the fish from time to time are seemingly greater.

Possibly the reason for this difference according to the temperature is that as the rate of metabolism increases, so does the development of milt or ova. This will result in an increase in the small amount of body waste, and growing adjustments required of some of the internal tissue, which may call for some slight physical exercise to assist the processes.

These spells of greater awareness of the salmon that are settled in pools apparently put them into much the same mood as fish while running, or immediately preceding and following such activity; and are clearly responsible for a great deal of the sport throughout the major part of the season.

Examination of the productive fishing days alone, however, fails to isolate some of the extremely simple yet important facts that point to lines of further investigation. But comparisons with very poor days put these items into relief.

No-one will dispute that the worst possible clear-water conditions are when there is a cold, dry, east wind with little or no cloud throughout the twentyfour hours and almost continuous sunshine during the day. The air temperature will almost certainly be higher than that of the water and, therefore, what is sometimes regarded as being troublesome in that respect—the air being colder than the water—does not apply. Due to the dryness of the air, evaporation takes place all the time and the consequent loss of calorific heat by the water prevents the effects of the sunshine and warmer atmosphere from raising its temperature above that of the air. Also it is characteristic that the atmospheric pressure is high, often very much so.

At the other extreme there is the situation in summer when the sky is overcast, the air very hot and humid, and the atmospheric pressure low: in other words, the torpid conditions that often lead up to thunderstorms. Evaporation is negligible, but since the water temperature is usually very high by the time the sultry conditions have got established, further warming of the water is not usually very pronounced.

These examples show that both high and low barometric pressure, and high and low relative humidity of the atmosphere, can be associated with the worst conditions in which to expect response from the fish, although the water temperature relative to the air temperature is not behaving in a way that can be said to be inimical to sport. There is, however, one strong similarity between the two positions: most of the principal factors remain very static indeed throughout the period.

When the adverse conditions are compared broadly with the very varied kinds of weather that can produce satisfactory sport, it is noticed immediately that the taking times occur when some change is taking place. Either the air temperature is changing appreciably and the water temperature to a lesser degree, or some variation is taking place in the relative humidity of the atmosphere or the barometric pressure. Hence it can be seen that no specific values of the individual factors can bring about the change in the humour of the salmon.

These observations suggest that examples of a variety of taking times should be examined with a view to establishing whether any particular direction of change of any of the factors so far mentioned is common to all cases. But only a brief survey is necessary to show that movements either way can each bring about the responsive mood. Nevertheless, a pattern does emerge. Just as the rises and falls in the air temperature are, in turn, associated with the morning and evening taking times on a pleasant summer day, falls in the barometric pressure and relative humidity of the atmosphere are for the better when their readings have been high, whereas rises are needed when they have been very low.

Yet, to repeat, no specific readings that may be reached in this way can account for the phenomenon of the responsive humour of the salmon. Therefore it appears that basically none of the factors so far considered can directly, either separately or jointly, influence *in their own right* the rather sudden, short term increase in the mental and physical alertness of the fish. This suggests that the only item that appears to remain, the nature of the salmon's oxygen supply, which is affected by the other factors, is the key to the problem.

Salmon Taking Times attempted to propound the oxygen theory. The original manuscript was written over twelve years ago – my first effort at writing – and since then some aspects that were confusing have been elucidated, simply by widening the context. Details will be given in the text.

First, the principles involved must be enumerated. The maximum concentration of dissolved oxygen possible in water is when it is at its densest – 39°F – and any rise in the temperature from that point means a reduced capacity. Hence, if water at 50°F is at saturation point or thereabout, which will normally be the case on the majority of good rivers, a rise in the temperature automatically means that a slight super-saturation will ensue, thus giving the fish an increased availability of oxygen. And it is this boost that the theory suggests can be responsible for promoting the taking humour. But too free a supply and too much unnecessary exertion are not in the best interests of the fish. Therefore, any tendency towards excess makes the fish lie very quietly and keep its respirations down at a suitable level. Later a decline in the water temperature reduces the availability of oxygen to the level that once again encourages alertness. In turn this gives way to the position when the cooling water is tending to be below saturation point, thus reducing the availability to the fish to less than the level that was rather exhilarating, so to speak, and the salmon resumes its very inactive mood.

At the start of a pleasant spring day when the salmon appear to be disinterested, the angler will hope for the beneficial slight lift in the water temperature. But the warming up of the atmosphere cannot affect the water sufficiently if it is impeded by a lot of evaporation. Low relative humidity of the atmosphere and high barometric pressure are sure to mean a lot of evaporation and poor prospects both of sport with the salmon and hatches of fly for the trout. Nymphs need the slight boost of oxygen to assist the metamorphosis into winged flies.

The favourable conditions are when the relative humidity of the atmosphere is only slightly below maximum – this does not mean that there will be any sense of dampness in the air – and the pressure is rather on the low side, but definitely not very high. There are no strict levels for the figures concerned, but generally speaking, the barometer does not look good at above 30in. and the hygrometer should read above 85 per cent to be favourable. However, after a little experience, instruments are quite unnecessary: one easily judges the right conditions, or perhaps more easily, the wrong conditions.

Translated into homely terms, the unfavourable weather factors make for a *good drying day* for the washing, while the promising day is what the gardner recognizes as a *good growing day*.

Before going any further, however, there should be no misunderstanding about the adequacy of the oxygen supply at all normal times. If the water gets warmer than about 65°F, the oxygen may tend to get less than is really suitable for the comfort of the salmon. But with that exception, the perpetual aeration of the good salmon river and the way in which the vegetation – the practically invisible growth on all the pebbles as well as the easily seen weeds – is caused to give off oxygen by photosynthesis during the daytime, together ensure that the concentration of dissolved oxygen in the water is kept at, or close to saturation point at all times, whether the temperature is rising or falling. And if a salmon is shocked out of the state of maximum rest at other than a taking time, the availability of oxygen is fully suitable for the physical well-being of the fish.

Some explanation is also required concerning the taking times that occur when the water temperature has made a smooth, steady drop from an unseasonably high reading, which is liable to happen at any time after the spring equinox. In the first place, the start of the rise in temperature that caused the situation would probably produce good sport, but soon the continued rise would put the fish off owing to too great an availability of oxygen. At the top of the temperature curve, the super-saturation would cease. Then, as the fall began, there would be a tendency for the availability to be on the low side as the increasing capacity of the water to absorb oxygen was constantly working to reach saturation point again. But there comes a position when the newly increased oxygen content, although not at super-saturation point, produces a greater availability to the fish than for some considerable time. And this, apparently, acts as the boost to put them into a taking mood.

The situation when the water temperature is below 39°F is rather different from that of the more temperate times when the water is above the point of its highest density. In *Salmon Taking Times* I made it clear that I could not then attempt to explain the phenomenon. My difficulty was this. The oxygen availability at these low temperatures in all reasonably normal conditions is undoubtedly higher throughout the twentyfour hours than is ever required by the salmon in their low metabolic state. Yet practical experience shows quite clearly that well defined, good taking periods are brought about by the same kind of overhead conditions and upward trend of the temperature of the water that are the most commonly required at above 39°F. It must also be remembered that rises in temperature below 39°F do not result in super-saturation of oxygen as they do when above that figure.

It is incredibly difficult to get apposite detailed

information in this subject, but I am much indebted to one scientist whose general observations made it clear to me that I had not been paying close enough attention to the question of the metabolism of the fish.

The observable overall behaviour of the salmon up to the time when it will pass through white water and leap over high obstacles at 42°F, compared with that during the rest of the rise in the water temperature up to the summer level, gives a good indication of what the graph of the metabolic rate of the fish must look like. Up to 42°F the rate of increase can be judged to be very much steeper than it is thereafter.

Apparently, therefore, the sequence at the lower temperatures is that the increase in the water temperature causes a sufficiently big increase in the rate of metabolism to arouse the salmon and put it into a taking humour. This increased rate of metabolism will, of course, automatically result in some increase in the amount of oxygen absorbed. And although the increase in the rate of metabolism will probably be seen to be the prime factor, the phenomenon can reasonably be allowed to remain as an associated part of the oxygen theory without having to give it a separate label.

Perhaps it will have been noticed that there appears to be a contradiction. At low temperatures the salmon can remain completely inactive when the availability of oxygen is higher than required, while it is claimed that at higher temperatures the establishment of a higher availability arouses the salmon. The explanation of this also gives added support to the theory.

The chosen lie of the salmon in the low temperatures is in an extremely gentle flow where the least intake of oxygen will occur at the particular respiratory rate, consistent, of course, with a minimum expenditure of effort. Apart from absolutely still water – which has several physical disadvantages for the fish – there is no other kind of lie in the river which would enable a reduction in oxygen intake to be made. Therefore it can be said that variations in the respiratory rate are the only acceptable means of obviating an unduly high intake of oxygen.

At temperatures above 39°F the salmon normally lies in rather faster flows. It seems that when in the inactive mood, the three-way balance between the rate of respiration, the rate of the flow, and the availability of oxygen, that will produce the correct intake, is unconsciously maintained. And the advent of an increase in the availability automatically produces a greater intake of oxygen. This puts the salmon into the alert mood. Later, after the fish has perhaps indulged in some head-and-tail rises and the oxygen supply becomes excessive, the fish will move a little to the side into a gentler flow; or if the excess becomes acute, it will desert the current altogether and seek the shelter of a deep, quiet lie. Eventually, after the temperature has started to decline, the salmon will go back to its original lie and probably perform a few head-and-tail rises again. And after a further decline in the temperature it will become very quiet, presumably back into the state of maximum rest.

All this procedure has been observed in minute detail on many occasions and careful monitoring of all the factors at the time has confirmed the claims of the oxygen theory.

It will be seen that the two apparently contradictory positions − the rise and the fall in the water temperature − are not only reconcilable: they show how improbable it is that any other factor than the availability of oxygen could have a feasible influence covering both situations satisfactorily.

With some hesitance I feel I ought to mention another matter in connection with water temperatures. The natural division for fishing between the cold water phase and the transitional period is, of course, 42°F; the temperature which *frees* the salmon from severe restrictions in their scope to travel. And from most practical points of view, 39°F can be forgotten excepting when it has to be mentioned for the sake of accuracy. But there is an interesting possibility about this densest point of water which unfortunately I can only call a suspicion. My monitoring has suggested strongly – without there being any obvious yardstick with which to prove it – that water below 39°F is less resistant to a rise in temperature than it is when the reading is above that figure. In other words, when the air is a little warmer than the water and other factors are not unfavourable, the water gains calorific heat faster than at higher temperatures. There would appear to be some slight reasons why this should be so, but I am not competent to do more than speculate very vaguely about them. However, if there were any substance in this suggestion, it would help to explain why a taking time comes more quickly than one would expect in unpleasant but not unfavourable wintry conditions.

VIII. Summary of the oxygen theory in practice
1. Water temperatures from the minimum to 39°F
A slight rise in the water temperature puts the salmon into a responsive mood, due to the beneficial effect on the metabolic rate and an increased intake of oxygen.

At the start of the day, the air temperature may well be below that of the water, but this is immaterial providing the atmosphere does warm up to a higher reading than the water, and the relative humidity and pressure of the atmosphere allow the water temperature to rise a little.

A very raw, damp airstream that is just a few degrees less cold than the water is well capable of bringing about the necessary improvement. Similarly, good sport can easily eventuate towards the middle of the day when the river is fringed with ice and it has been snowing all morning.

Quite often on a breezy day when the barometer is tending high, the air may not seem to be unfavourably cold, but the salmon remain stiff throughout what should be the best period. Towards evening the breeze will probably fade away and immediately the air feels a little softer. A check will show that the atmospheric pressure has dropped a little and the relative humidity is higher. Such a situation is very favourable indeed for a spell of quick sport.

The deterioration from relatively mild conditions to colder, drier weather is very unfavourable. It is rare at the low temperatures however, that there is absolutely no chance of catching an odd salmon. The slow-moving lure at eye level that threatens to bump a fish on the nose may well be taken. In warmer water, the salmon would probably prefer to move away, but with the metabolism at a low pitch, it seems that it is easier to deal with the lure by seizing it in the mouth, no doubt with the intention of spitting it out after giving it a good squeeze.

Most probably the eye of the fish operates with the same net result as the human ear: i.e. that it sees everything, but only arouses conscious response in the brain when something startling occurs. Also the lateral line is so sensitive to vibrations that it is unlikely that a large fly or spinner could approach dangerously close to the nose without the fish getting adequate warning, although it may otherwise be oblivious to everything around.

2. Water temperatures from 39°F upwards

In the forenoon, a slight rise in the temperature of the water will increase the availability of oxygen and put the salmon into an alert, responsive mood. A continuation of this trend may result in excessive availability, in which case the fish will go off the take and remain very quiet throughout the heat of the day. Later there will be excellent prospects of sport after the water has started to cool down again.

No doubt enough has already been said about the typical kinds of weather that are favourable and adverse, for there to be no further difficulty regarding conditions that point clearly one way or the other. In conditions that seem to lean neither way, one will usually persevere as a matter of course, but then the thing to watch for is, of course, some positive change. This should remove any doubt about the short term prospects.

When the water temperature gets high, say above 60°F, the state of the atmosphere overnight is the best guide to the prospects on the following day. If the atmosphere is rather dry and the pressure at all high, the air temperature will show a substantial drop during the hours of darkness. The morning sunshine will warm the air up quickly, but due to the high rate of evaporation that will take place, the rise in the water temperature will be small and slow. The pattern that can then be expected will be similar to that of a much cooler day — a spell of sport in the mid-morning and another one in the evening when the atmosphere begins to cool down again.

If the atmosphere during the night remains rather warm, however, the humidity will not be low and the pressure will not be high. Therefore, the morning sunshine will soon raise the temperature of the water. Consequently the best time to fish will probably be very soon after daybreak and it will be unlikely to last for longer than about an hour. And the taking time in the evening will be delayed until very close to dusk.

Daytime sport is improbable when the atmosphere is consistently hot and humid, and as mentioned earlier, a good drop in the temperature is wanted before any big improvement in the response of the fish can be expected. Such conditions, however, which usually include an overcast sky, are often very favourable for fly fishing for salmon during the hours of darkness. In fast, shallow, streamy water above deep holding-pools, a medium sized silhouette pattern — say a Low Water no. 5 Blue Charm — fished subsurface will sometimes bring hectic sport. The fish leave the deep, steady water to which they have been confined during the daytime for the well-aerated water, and are then alert and interested enough to take very freely.

The other particularly good circumstances for night fishing are when both the level of the river and the atmospheric conditions are favourable for the salmon to be running, but following a day when the fish were inactive for some reason – possibly the weather being too sunny. This situation may well happen when there is some bright moonlight. The best spots for sport are the major resting-places just below and above stretches of hard going, especially those involving travel through a lot of white water. Smaller flies may then take fish, but there is seldom any true need to go below a Low Water no. 6. And again, the silhouette pattern is the best choice.

It is noteworthy that the sport with salmon during the hot, humid night is very much the reverse of what happens with the school sea-trout. For them, a slight drop in the temperature is wanted towards dusk: then the flies and moths come out and the trout feed greedily and well into the night. But when the atmosphere remains too heavy and close for the flies, the trout are very dour, too. A large lure fished slowly, near to the bottom, may then take a big sea trout, possibly due to aggressive reaction, but medium sized sea-trout flies fished subsurface are much more likely to catch a salmon than a sea trout.

3. Autumn fishing

Salmon that run fresh from the sea very close to spawning time have no need to follow a pattern of behaviour that is based on conservation of energy. Their prime need is to reach suitable beds of gravel for spawning as expeditiously as water conditions will allow. The result is that the fish move upstream almost ceaselessly unless they are compelled to stop by a big overnight drop in the air temperature when the water is low enough for this to have a marked effect. Even when semi-resident in a big pool, however, the fish tend to move at short intervals from one lie to another a little upstream, but such changes of position are made along the bottom, of course, not on the surface as when engaged in a full-scale running operation.

Seemingly the salmon are fully alert most of the time: indeed, non-taking moods are rare and seldom last long.

Naturally, a big, coloured water or a gale can put a stop to fishing. Also, when the fish are running hard there are undoubtedly tactical problems to be solved that may be far from easy. But apart from such matters, it could not be said that there are any times that are outstandingly better than others, which point is borne out by the records.

Certainly the angler who is only familiar with the habits of springers and summer salmon should adopt an entirely different view for any autumn fishing he may do. Perseverance whenever conditions seem tolerable is undoubtedly the best policy.

When reviewing this statement of the taking time theory, the concept that the salmon requires to be *awakened* may seem to suggest the question – why should this not be done by physical means? It will be appreciated, however, that this is a very old idea. Early in the season when the fish proved to be disinterested some anglers used to swim a dog through the pool in the belief that it did some good. In warmer weather when sport is quiet, some fly fishers consider that it improves their chances to follow down the pools behind a spinner using a big lure. On some fly-only rivers, the gillie – usually at his own suggestion – goes down the water first fishing an over-large, gaudy fly, and the rod follows using what is thought to be the correct size and pattern for the prevailing conditions.

Obviously the salmon requires to be aroused without scaring it, or causing any distraction that will be at the expense of interest in the lure. And if this can be done, there may be a fair chance that a fish will take. But I consider that if the state of conditions is not suitable for a natural taking time, the salmon will rapidly resume their previous inactive frame of mind.

Further references will be made to aspects of taking times in the chapters dealing with practical fishing, but before closing this present section, several other related matters should be mentioned that could not conveniently be fitted in earlier.

Two kinds of situation can arise when sport is unusally poor for a protracted period. During some seasons, wintry conditions take a firm grip after the arrival of the early runs of salmon and persist for an abnormally long time. In the early stages, there are the usual small variations in temperature and sport progresses satisfactorily. But eventually, after there has been no relief from the lower bracket of temperatures for several weeks, it becomes hardly worth fishing. Naturally, no new runs of fish occur pending a suitable height of water and relatively mild temperatures; also the resident salmon see a great deal of all the suitable kinds of lure. However, those disadvantages do not seem to be enough to account for the almost complete lack of response, especially when it is remembered that the salmon are naturally in a comparatively dreamy mood and not nearly as sensitive to the interference of anglers as they can be later in the season. Ultimately there may be a softening in the weather, but no worthwhile improvement in response takes place until there has been a good water and the fish have moved upstream to fresh pools. Then sport picks up and may soon return to normal.

The reason that suggests itself is that the enduring of an over-prolonged period of low metabolism is debilitating to the salmon and it requires a spell at a higher rate before its normal, healthy humour can be restored. One scientist has expressed the opinion that UDN started as a result of the arctic conditions during the early months of 1963 and the reasoning seems to be sound.

Fortunately the second case, although much more frequent, is not usually so serious. It is very seldom that salmon will take when the river is rising in spate, either steadily or quickly. During the pre-spate phase of the rise of clear water before the true spate-water arrives, the fish will often take remarkably readily; but that ceases as soon as the colour begins to appear, although it may be only slight. It is well known that salmon do not like a lot of suspended matter in the water and seek shelter from it, but difficulties of that sort do not explain every occasion. However, the thermometer will usually reveal that there has been a sudden drop in the temperature of the water amounting to several degrees.

In normal circumstances, changes in the water temperature are so gradual that, judging by fishing results, they cause no discomfort and have no adverse effect on the fish. But a sudden drop evidently requires some hours for the fish to adjust.

However, after a period of numerous rises and falls in the level of the river in quick succession, the fish may require several days in which to recuperate. This can cause some despondency among anglers, and it is sometimes suggested that the fish concerned will become stale without ever resuming normal behaviour; in other words, they will become permanently non-takers. This impression is probably caused by the tendency of the salmon to move some way upstream as their first act on recovering a good humour. But this is not simply a local problem. It applies to a big part of the river, if not to all the populated areas. And since the new arrivals in a pool have almost certainly been behaving just like their predecessors, yet soon prove not to be non-takers when conditions are favourable, the pessimism is seen to be groundless.

A problem which may involve the oxygen theory is that of the well known peculiar behaviour of salmon on some occasions when an angler resorts to the use of the prawn. The fish may ignore the bait just as they would any other lure, or they may at times take it quite freely. But there have been many authentic reports of a mass exodus from a pool as soon as a prawn entered the water. I have not witnessed such an event myself, no doubt because I have very rarely seen prawn fishing being practised. However, the oxygen theory suggests a seemingly reasonable explanation for such a remarkable reaction.

The normal disinterested and taking moods would account for the uneventful and responsive periods. And it seems quite likely that when the availability of oxygen is decidedly excessive, the salmon could be heady and take fright at the sight of the prawn. The abundance of oxygen does not, of course, restrict physical exertion in any way, and may actively encourage exaggerated reaction to the sudden scare.

A suitable note on which to leave this subject of the taking humour of the salmon is provided by the fresh-run fish carrying sea lice that is caught fifty miles or more from the estuary on a tiny subsurface fly. The rise and interception of the fly are as neat and stylish as could be imagined, although the fight may show some indication that the fish is tired. Yet all the changing scenes and incidents that it must have experienced during the busy two days or so of travel had not dulled its mentality in the slightest. The tiny illusion appeared and the reflexes produced the perfectly co-ordinated feat of meeting it at the most propitious point with the least effort, but with a wonderfully picturesque show of some of the salmon's most fascinating, characteristic behaviour.

The importance of the supply of oxygen in such a case requires no stressing. Nor does the fact that the influence of the elements is vital in this respect. Even so, the value of the theory does not depend on the accuracy of the nominal findings in respect of the chemical and physiological happenings. Its real worth lies in the establishment of a common denominator for the weather and water factors on a seasonal basis, which is in full conformity with the records and one's own personal fishing experience.

2 Heavy Spinning

I. Strategy

Early season spinning before the temperature of the water has risen permanently above about 42°F is, in principle, the most simple problem of the entire season's fishing. When properly settled, the salmon are certain to be lying in a fairly gentle flow in deepish water. The undisputed policy is to give them a good look at the large lure and a very easy opportunity to seize it.

The only remaining question on the average day is whether the fish will rise a little way, say a foot or two, to meet the lure as it swings round in the flow: if they will, it is both the easiest and most effective way of fishing. On poor days, the best chances are with the lure at eye level, but then it may escape notice of the fish unless it approaches very closely and in the correct position.

In practice, however, heavy spinning requires much more detailed attention and personal skill than superficial appearances would suggest. The difficulties arise through the fact that the water surrounding the pockets of comfortable flow that suit the fish may be quite turbulent, particularly in the upper levels through which the line must pass. Hence the basic requirement is the capability to maintain maximum control over the *line* in all situations, so that the lure, in turn,

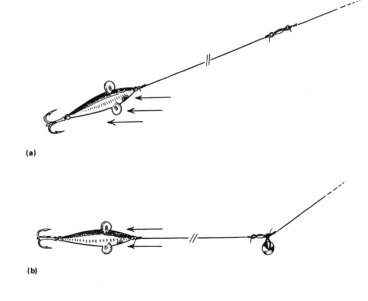

Devon fished without lead (a); effect of lead on the line (b)
FIG. 1

can be made to do what is required of it.

It is much nicer to cast and fish with no lead on the trace on the rare occasions when this can be done without incurring faulty presentation of the lure. But in deepish water it is almost impossible to fish a wood or plastic Devon on a level keel without the assistance of a lead to keep the line in control, despite the fact that the best of these baits are weighted towards the head. And if the line pulls the revolving bait into the *head-up* position, too much of its surface area is exposed to the force of the current, thus resulting in forward and upward pressure: this may take the lure completely out of control just at the crucial moment when it is reaching taking range of a salmon (See Fig. 1).

No amount of skill can compensate for the lack of a lead when unpredictable variations in the current at all levels affect the line to the possible extent of destroying the

effectiveness of the lure. Whenever there is the slightest
doubt, a lead should be used without hesitation. And there
are so many ways in which leads can fulfil valuable functions
that they require to be enumerated.

II. The functions of leads
The lead should simply be regarded as a useful division of the
total weight required to fish at the depth in question — not as
an additional weight — and its primary function is to slow the
bait down so that it fishes correctly at the speed organized by
the angler.

If all the weight required is concentrated in the bait itself,
attempts to slow it down are inefficient owing to the direct
pull of the line at a steep angle. Also, when the heavy bait
enters a pocket of slacker flow, it has a tendency to plummet
down onto the bottom.

When part of the weight is external, a lighter lure can be
used, and the lead works like a moving anchor. Increased
pressure of the water on the line or on the lead has a
minimum of effect and the bait continues to fish correctly.
In spots where there is a reduction in the force of the flow,
the balancing effect of the resistance of the line and the pull
of the revolving lure, help to prevent the lead from dropping
suddenly. But if it does bump the bottom here and there, this
will rarely spoil the performance of the lure.

The lead also makes for increased efficiency in covering
more water correctly with each cast.

When a Devon enters the water without an external lead,
the resistance of the fins as it sinks causes it to spin, thus
reducing the rate of fall considerably, and exposing most of
the length to the force of the flow. In deep water with a fast
flow for most of the way down, the consequent loss of
ground before fishing level is reached cannot be less than
several yards. This means more line submerged and reduced
control. Then there is nothing one can do if the bait swings
round faster than wished and only fishes correctly for a short

distance on the nearside of the river.

The lead on its own would obviously drop very much more quickly and vertically than the unaided Devon. And even though it has to drag the lighter lure after it, there is a big saving in the ground lost before fishing level is reached. Then, with less submerged line and greater resistance generally to the flow, the bait can be made to fish correctly throughout its course.

Manoeuvres that are practically impossible otherwise can be executed very efficiently through the use of a lead.

Sudden, deep little depressions in the bed of the river often make very good lies. If line is given at the appropriate moment to let the unaided lure drop to the right level, it will dive either head or tail first and will probably have drifted below the fish before recovering the right poise to be fishing properly. With the external lead, the change of level is achieved with a minimum, or no loss of correct behaviour by the bait.

The lead allows the easy execution of such manoeuvres as leading the lure round large boulders and, in steady water, drawing the bait upstream from behind the fish and thus into its taking zone, which sometimes proves to be effective.

From the point of view of convenience and economy alone, leads are well worth their place. With a suitable range of leads, only one weight of Devon is required in each of the larger sizes. The same bait can be used practically everywhere with varying weights of leads. But if numerous variations in weight in each size of Devon have to be carried, it is a nuisance.

Anti-kink leads in the shape of drilled lead-balls with spring-wire clips are very effective and are available in all sizes. They are quickly attached to the top eye of the ball-bearing swivel, and since more than one can be used at the same time, it is possible to make very small additions or reductions in weight when desired.

III. Evaluation of types of baits
Different types have different characteristics both visually and in physical performance.

There is a tendency among less experienced anglers to regard the different types as merely optional alternatives. This is a serious undervaluation, because the help that can be got from the purposeful exploitation of the differences is an essential part of spinning.

Without saying at the moment that it is the most important, the Devon Minnow will be mentioned first because it can be used as a yardstick by which to judge other types.

1. The Devon Minnow
With malleable fins, the rate of spin can be adjusted and this is one of the most valuable features of the Devon. Too fast a spin tends to put the pattern to a discount, therefore the rate should be kept to the lowest that will give the bait the correct degree of buoyancy. In a poor flow, the rate of spin required tends to be too high for the best visual results unless the bait is reasonably light. Therefore the standard of weight most desirable is that which will fish correctly at a slow rate of spin, and can be used with more external weight when required. Wooden Devons, preferably with additional weight in the head, are popularly thought to be the best compromise in the larger sizes. Rather heavier plastic Devons, again weighted towards the head, are also very useful, but particularly in the next smaller sizes suitable for fishing rather less deep water when the temperature is in the higher part of the bracket. Then either the wooden or plastic Devon will often fish correctly without the use of an external lead.

In the deeper water without a lead, the Devon is rather easily pushed towards the side of the river owing to the large surface area exposed to the thrust of the current on the side of the fastest flow. For this reason, some meticulous anglers believe in having duplicate sets: the clockwise spin for fishing from the right bank and the anti-clockwise for the left bank. This undoubtedly helps a little and, of course, a little help may make all the difference on some occasions between catching a fish and failure. Another view taken by some anglers is that the standard Devon is too symmetrical and tends to lack life-like movement. The enthusiasts build up their own Devons in plastic wood and almost automatically this results in a vibratory kind of wobble, which they consider to be important.

Once the fish is hooked, the Devon is extremely efficient. The way the shell moves away from the hook-hold prevents any leverage and the number of fish lost is probably a smaller percentage than with almost any other bait.

2. The Golden Sprat

The preserved Golden Sprat fished on a natural bait spinning-flight has rather a floppy spin compared with the Devon, and this does seem to be an advantage when extra impact is wanted. It requires quite a good flow to make the bait revolve satisfactorily and there is a tendency for it to get pushed aside by the current more quickly; hence it cannot always be fished quite as slowly as a Devon.

However, the Golden Sprat does not lack devotees and some of them are most fastidious about the way it should be mounted on the flight, no doubt with a view to making it spin reasonably smoothly so that it is not difficult for the lazy fish to seize.

3. The wobbling spoon

The great feature of this lure is its inherent ability to fish correctly on an even keel and very slowly without the need for any very skilful manipulation by the angler — a tight line is all that is needed.

The wobble is, or should be, entirely fore and aft. This up-and-down *beating* of the water, together with the fact that so little surface area is exposed to side pressure, helps the bait to cling to the current and swing round to the side much more slowly than any other lure.

It is a good plan to test each wobbling spoon by watching its action in the current when held in one position on a short line. If there is any tendency for it to lean sideways when wobbling, it should be put aside for use only as a fast-moving lure. It is difficult to discover what causes some of the spoons to be faulty, but they cannot be corrected, and the loss of performance is too great to be acceptable. Fortunately only occasional ones behave unsatisfactorily.

Some makes conveniently have the weight stamped on the bait. The 3½ in. spoon weighing $^5/8$ oz will fish round in a medium flow, unaided by a lead, at a constant depth which can be regulated by the angler on the basis of the amount he allows it to sink before applying the pressure that will make it start working in the current. Similarly, it will behave perfectly at a shallow depth without showing any tendency to break surface. This makes it an excellent lure for running fish.

This remarkable performance is, of course, governed by the ratio of the surface area to the weight. Some of the smaller sizes are relatively more heavy for their size and tend to drop to the bottom unless their water speed is increased by the recovery of line. The one-ounce 3½in. model will fish round slowly at a big depth in a heavy current; and with the addition of a small lead on the trace, it will cover lies correctly in the deepest, heaviest flows in which salmon are ever likely to be found.

For most normal fishing at a good depth, the 3 ½ in. $^5/8$ oz size with the occasional help of a small lead is the most versatile model.

The excellent features of the wobbling spoon, however, are not without their unfortunate consequences. The less-skilled angler tries a Devon – probably without a lead – and soon realizes that he has insufficient control over it. When he substitutes a wobbling spoon, he appreciates the improvement, perseveres, and eventually catches a fish. Repeated experiences of this sort ultimately tempt him to become an habitual user of the wobbling spoon.

But circumstances are not always best suited to the extra impact made by the wobbling spoon as compared with the Devon. There are many days when continuous fishing on a beat with Devons for several hours does not put the fish off too much and everyone has a reasonable chance of sport. Once down a pool with the wobbling spoon on some occasions, however, is enough to put the fish down for the rest of the taking period, especially if it is not used very thoughtfully. Inept use of any lure that has the capability of making maximum impact should certainly be discouraged.

4. The jointed plug

The ability of this lure to dive deeply when held firmly, or drawn slightly against a powerful current, makes it invaluable for searching for salmon in very confined spots where there is not enough clearance for the normal approach of a Devon or a wobbling spoon. On rivers containing a large number of such lies, the lure is very popular; but it is not seen very much on the big rivers with large, unobstructed pools. Nevertheless, both articulate and one-piece models can be very useful for running fish in the gliding type of water on all rivers. The particular feature of the plug in this respect is that it will fish correctly in a rather slower flow than is best suited to the wobbling spoon.

Articulate plugs require testing in the same way as wobbling spoons. Any tendency for the wobble fore and aft of the joint to turn the bait on its side detracts from its deep diving ability; also its controllability near to the surface suffers, and it should not be used. Regular plug fishers complain that too big a proportion of those purchased turn out to be faulty in performance.

Above top: The Wye, most famous of English salmon rivers and a notable big fish river, seen here at Upper Bigsweir

Above: Rapid water on the Usk.

Above top: The Errocht Pool on the Awe. Best in the latter part of the season.

Above: The Hampshire Avon at Ibsley: its chalkstream character makes it untypical among salmon rivers.

IV. Rods, reels and lines

The outfit is not complete without both the free-spool multiplier and the fixed-spool reel. With strong lines of about 20 lb test, and heavy baits from around ¾ oz and up, the multiplier will cast considerably further than the fixed-spool reel, which is a decided advantage on the larger rivers. On the other hand, with a line not exceeding 14 lb test, the fixed-spool reel will make quite long casts with baits down to about $1/3$ oz. Also, the fixed-spool reel is more versatile in coping with certain manoeuvres requiring some line to be payed out. According to the design of the reel and whether it is operated by the right or left hand, the line – after the cast has been made – can be picked-up on the tip of the forefinger, or locked by dropping the finger onto the rim of the spool, instead of operating the bale-arm. Then, while the bait is being fished round – without any winding of the reel handle, of course – line can be allowed to run from the spool and then be checked again at will. No problem of over-runs has to be considered and the manoeuvres can be performed without the distraction of having to watch the reel.

The type of line must be considered, though, before one can decide which combinations are the most suitable.

Braided lines are much easier to see than monofilament and this is an advantage in most styles of spinning. But the braided line causes more water resistance and this is practically always a disadvantage. Braided lines can also be said to be the most trouble-free for the multiplier. Many anglers are now using monifilament on this type of reel and it does seem to increase the range appreciably. Monofilament also has the advantage of not carrying as much water down to wet the hand and cause discomfort. But an over-run with monofilament can be an utterly hopeless tangle, whereas with braided line it can usually be sorted out without trying the patience too much. Over-runs should not occur, of course, but the better the reel, the worse the over-run if the bait happens to hit some obstruction at the beginning of the cast.

This is a risk from which very few anglers are entirely immune when the salmon are moving well and the time seems to be racing away far too quickly.

The fixed-spool reel, of course, performs the best with monofilament, which pleases most anglers despite the difficulty in seeing it clearly enough when the bait is fishing round.

After considering all the pros and cons, most anglers settle for a fixed-spool reel loaded with about 14 lb test monofilament and a multiplier carrying a 20 lb test line – monofilament if the individual is very brave and braided if he prefers to see his line better!

The only suitable rod for heavy spinning is popularly agreed to be a double-handed nine- or ten-footer – preferably the longer one. It requires enough power at the tip to maintain control of a heavy bait in fast water and to ensure deep hook penetration, but there should also be enough through action to ensure smooth casting with the multiplier.

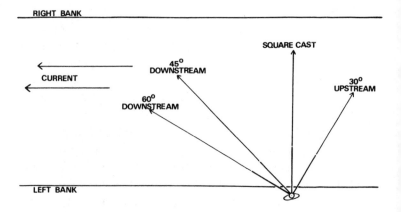

FIG. 2

V. The angle of the cast

There is the risk of confusion when the angle of the cast is stated in degrees upstream or downstream. The cast straight across the river is clearly at ninety degrees, but it is always called *square,* and thirty degrees downstream naturally implies that the angle is the offset from the square, and not the angle between the cast and the bank. Therefore all references to casting angles shortly to be made will be based on the square cast being the zero line (See Fig. 2).

VI. Tactics

With the river at normal winter level and the weather dull and raw, the salmon are unlikely to be very lively at the start of the day in January or early February. The plan therefore will be to begin fishing with the lure down at the eye level of the fish. On the big pools of the lower reaches of the early rivers, the bottom is usually fairly even without too many troublesome angular rocks or snags, and is very suitable for presenting the lure at very close quarters. If a pool is known to have a very irregular bottom, however, it should be saved for the occasions when the salmon show some willingness to rise a foot or two to meet the bait.

The basic essential now is to establish as quickly and accurately as possible the *angle of the optimum cast.* And the first step is to find bottom. A steady flow will suggest a 2¾in. Yellow Belly Devon, aided by a ¼ oz anti-kink lead, and a long throw is made at about 30° downstream. As soon as the bait is about to touch the water, the line is checked momentarily – with the thumb on the multiplier or the forefinger on the rim of the fixed-spool – and immediately afterwards the line is allowed to go free until the lead is felt to bump on the bottom. Now the clutch or bale-arm is engaged and the rod raised almost to the vertical, by which time the line should be tight onto the lead. Then, without any winding of the reel handle, the lure is allowed to swing round at its own speed (See Fig. 3).

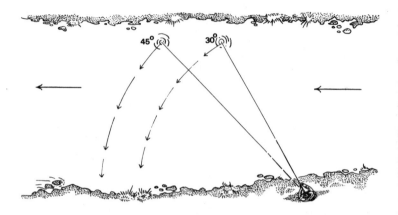

FIG. 3

If the speed of the lure is nice and steady, and judged to be right to give the salmon plenty of time to see it and take hold, if too the lead is felt to touch bottom two or three times during the traverse to the edge of the current, then no improvement could be suggested at that moment. The bait will be fishing correctly for the maximum distance that it is possible to arrange, and this produces the basis for a methodical, effective coverage of the pool. Some adjustments will have to be made where the current shows appreciable variations; but these are best explained by dealing with the situation when, for one of several reasons, the first cast does not give the desired results.

When the bait swings round at a reasonably suitable speed, but fails to touch bottom again after the original bottom-finding bump, it may be fishing considerably higher than is wanted at the time. Bearing in mind, however, that the fishing speed was thought to be about right, the addition of a $1/8$ oz lead should make the required correction. But if necessary, still more should be added until the occasional touch on the bottom is achieved.

Should the trial cast result in the lead bumping the bottom

too frequently and the movement appear to be rather slow, a slight reduction in the size of the lead would probably put matters right at that point. But if there is a good amount of rather faster water ahead, it is better to employ another remedy. A second throw should be made with no change of lead, and this time line should be retrieved very slowly while the bait is making its way across the river. This increases the water speed of the lead and bait, and should lift the lead sufficiently to prevent it from knocking the bottom too frequently. Also it should increase the rate at which the bait crosses very slightly, but would not make any appreciable difference to the amount of water covered after each cast.

So long as it is known that the bait is staying close to the bottom and not travelling across too quickly, slight variations in the rate of retrieve of line make very useful adjustments. This practice when fishing downstream and across is, of course, only correct when a long line is being fished. With a short line, any retrieve tends to lift the bait too much.

When the trial cast swings across the current too quickly, an extra lead would probably fail to slow it down sufficiently. Therefore a longer cast at a bigger angle (say 45°) should be tried. It will be seen from Fig. 3 that the distance fished by the bait will be the same, but the time taken to make the traverse will be longer owing to the decrease in the pressure of the current at the new angle; therefore the bait will travel more slowly. If this is then judged to be about right, the same adjustments as mentioned earlier in regard to altering the weight of the lead can be made if necessary.

Thus trial casts are made until the optimum angle is found. Once this is clearly established, the adjustments that can readily be made should enable the angler to fish the whole pool down very satisfactorily. And he will also have a good idea of what should be done in the way of altering the angle of casting or varying the weight of the lead if he should decide later that it would be better to fish with the bait a foot or so clear of the bottom.

Changes of two or three inches in the level of the river do not make much difference in these big pools to the flow at the bottom in the spots where the fish lie. The strength of the surface flow alters a great deal, however, and the data produced on one day concerning the optimum angle of the cast should only be considered to be an approximate guide for another apparently similar occasion.

An obviously faster flow, of course, requires a different appraisal for the trial cast. It may be thought necessary to make the first cast at 50° downstream with a 3½ in. Devon and a ½ oz anti-kink lead. If that fishes round too quickly, it will probably then be thought wisest to resort to the wobbling spoon without delay. In a clear water, however, it may be advisable to use the Black and Gold for a good trial period before deciding to risk the more striking patterns.

The drill for finding the right balance for fishing near the surface for running salmon with the wobbling spoon or the articulated plug is just the same in principle as the method for establishing the optimum angle of cast for deep fishing. Of course, the lure is given no time to sink when the trial cast is made, and as much line as possible is held clear of the water. Once it has been found how to make the lure work more or less on the surface of the water, it simply means either lowering the rod a little, or adding a small amount of weight, and the correct fishing level should be ensured.

In the upper part of the cold water bracket and during the transitional period, spinning downstream and across with the heavy tackle is often very successful in the rather less deep water that the fish then favour. Indeed, as early as January when the river is high following a relatively mild, wet spell, the shallower stretches of the lower reaches of the rivers where the flow is not too strong can be the most productive. At such times, of course, there may be travelling fish, runners that have halted for a short rest, and resident salmon that will not move until the level of the river drops, when the water will probably cool down to a more seasonable temperature.

Sport in the shallower water will frequently be the best with the bait fishing well clear of the bottom — as much as two or three feet. When there is some colour in the water, the lure is undoubtedly more easily seen at a high angle of sight. This can apply, of course, with the lure at only about two feet above the bottom and it is probably better not to expect the salmon to rise any more than the minimum amount required to ensure the greater impact of the lure as seen against the lightest background in the existing field of view.

In clear water conditions any willingness of the salmon to rise two or three feet is also an indication that the lure should be a little smaller and fished slightly faster: 2¼in. to 2½in. is usually about right.

Naturally one has to think in terms of broad averages when planning to fish at a given distance from the bottom and it depends largely on good judgment to discover the most effective procedure. Nevertheless, the same system of trial casts and making adjustments when the optimum angle has been found will usually be far more reliable than making spot changes without a routine.

VII. Signals from the salmon

The very gentle take of a fish that results simply in the line appearing to stop is a very good indication that the lure was fishing entirely suitably in all respects for the immediate circumstances. A heavy, snatchy take may have one of several meanings. Obviously the fish did not make a smooth, easy interception and drop gently back to its lie. This may have been because the lure did not make sufficient impact and was seen rather late, or it may have been moving rather too quickly. And if it was the image of the lure that was at fault, either the size or the colour could have been responsible. A re-examination of one's assessment of all the factors should produce some good pointer to the most likely fault, and this warning should certainly be heeded. One snatchy take could well mean that other fish had seen the lure and failed to respond to it.

Mostly when spinning with the heavy tackle, the bait will fish itself out quite a long distance downstream from the position of the rod – too far away to see if a salmon had followed it. But it is quite common for an angler to report that a fish had followed his bait almost to his feet. Primarily this is a splendid indication that the fish are not in a dour mood and that with more suitable presentation, sport should be very good. In abstract it is always difficult to suggest what was at fault when there are so many equally important details involved. But at least it can be said that the bait must have created an illusion that had been seen. And since the fish had had the energy to follow it, it would seem unlikely that the presentation had been too high in the water, or too fast moving. This suggests that either the same bait should be fished a little higher in the water so that it would be seen less discerningly and not deter the salmon from completing the full reaction to the illusion as seen from its lie; or a bait should be substituted that would create a more vague image when fished exactly as before.

Salmon heading-and-tailing in the same spot more than once – which does sometimes happen at the low temperatures, especially during a calm spell towards evening – is also an excellent sign that the fish are probably in a most responsive mood. And, of course, a hatch of fly in the cold weather should be seen as a most encouraging event.

VIII. Hooking salmon

Some anglers find it difficult to resist striking quickly and firmly as soon as they feel any touch. And one of the oldest puzzles in fishing is the question as to how so many salmon manage to avoid getting hooked by the large treble.

The movements of the fish in the cold water are comparatively very slow and deliberate: this includes the ejection of the large Devon after it has been taken and no immediate strike is made. And probably the vital factor is that the grip the fish gets on the bait is very strong indeed, as shown by the way sprats get mutilated. All this suggests that the rapid strike fails to make the hook move in the mouth of the fish, and therefore at that moment, no penetration is effected. But the salmon feels the tug and its reaction is to spit the bait out, which coincides with the rebound of the line from the strike. Hence the bait is ejected in such a way that the treble has little chance to engage.

A much more reliable procedure is simply to hold firmly against the fish and allow it to put a good bend into the rod, by which time it should be well hooked. The continuous pressure ensures that as soon as the salmon begins to loosen its grip on the bait, the treble starts to move and penetrates before the jaws are fully opened in the effort to get rid of the now unwanted and probably objectionable item. And since the salmon usually turns and moves directly away from the pressure it feels, the hook-hold is often in the most secure place in the corner of the mouth.

Wobbling spoons tend to lose rather an excessive proportion of the number of fish they hook. This is probably due to the leverage of the metal against the jaw. A home-made modification seems to be a good improvement. The split ring holding the treble is detached from the bottom of the bait, and is joined to the top split ring with a length of very strong nylon or trace wire, so that the treble retains its original relative position to the spoon. Then a piece of soft copper wire is placed through the ring holding the treble and secured with a couple of twists round itself. The two ends of the wire are then placed through the bottom hole in the spoon and splayed out to operate like a split pin. The wire is so soft that when a fish is hooked, the treble easily becomes detached from the spoon, thus leaving a situation much the same as with a Devon.

IX. Tailing a salmon
A horizontal stroke with a tailer should be avoided. The tail

of the salmon bends easily from side to side and then there is nothing rigid to act as a buffer and actuate the noose. But the tail of the fish will not bend under the pressure of a vertical stroke of the tailer, and the strong muscle at the root of the tail checks the wire and operates the noose correctly. Used in this way, the tailer is a very reliable instrument.

When tailing a salmon by hand, the safe and convenient way is to grip with the forefinger and thumb towards the tail. Then, when the fish is held up and hangs vertically from the hand, the elbow and arm are in the correct, comfortable position to cope with a large weight without feeling any strain.

If the salmon is lifted with the thumb and forefinger towards the head, the tail muscles act as a wedge pushing into the hand and tending to open it from the weakest side of the grip. Also, in order to hold the fish up with its head clear of the ground, the elbow must be raised high and away from the body into a most uncomfortable and straining position.

3 Sunk-Line Fishing

Various adaptations of methods of fishing have been tried from time to time and some have apparently come to stay. This makes it necessary for the angler to remind himself that the true rôle of a method is to perform the duty which it is able to fulfil more readily and effectively than any other. And any shortcomings resulting from applications that change the purpose of the method should be clearly seen to be of no account in the context of the true rôle.

The outstanding feature of heavy spinning is that it is the best means of *mastering* the force of the flow so that large lures can be presented correctly. With orthodox sunk-line fishing the specialized performance is in *employing* the buoyancy of the current as the means by which large lures can be presented correctly.

When each is used to its best advantage, heavy spinning and orthodox sunk-line fishing are complementary to each other.

It so happens, however, that the true identity of fly fishing with the sunk-line has almost been lost — it is certainly very well concealed among a lot of alien practices.

The introduction of plastic-coated, fast-sinking lines could be said to have made the method more versatile, but this is not true in principle. It is certainly very nice to cast with a line that shoots so beautifully, but when it cuts down through the water with such ease and defeats the current, it also destroys the foundation upon which the character of the method depends.

The fly-only rule on some rivers has probably been the worst offender against the character of sunk-line fishing. When one has no option but to fish the fly rod and line in circumstances where heavy spinning is obviously the most effective method, the only sensible thing to do is, of course, to contrive to make the fly behave in exactly the same way as the spinning bait, no matter how it disfigures the visage of fly fishing.

This super-heavy sunk-line fishing does produce some big catches early in the season from the huge, deep pools, when the angler has the use of a boat and a gillie. But it would be surprising if it were otherwise when there is a big stock of willing takers. And it does not alter the fact that spinning is the most efficient and, in those conditions, the most enjoyable method.

However, the purpose here is not to condemn super-heavy fly fishing — on the contrary, it will be dealt with as sympathetically as it deserves. The intention is to attempt to ensure that the good standing of orthodox sunk-line fishing does not get obscured or overlooked, particularly by young salmon fishers in whose hands the future of the sport will eventually lie.

In the circumstances, this chapter will be divided into two parts.

ORTHODOX SUNK-LINE FISHING

I. Strategy
The area of the very obvious supremacy of the true sunk line is in those situations where lures up to the largest sizes are required to be fished close to the bottom, but it is necessary that they should be very light in weight. This often happens

when the river is around normal level and the water temperature is in the upper thirties or lower forties. In many pools with much irregularity in the depth and in the force of the flow, fishing near to the bottom with spinning tackle can result in the bait continually getting snagged. Apart from the nuisance, the lure fails to cover the lies properly and is shown to be incapable of doing so.

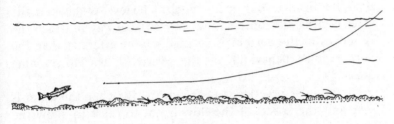

FIG. 4

With the sunk line, the principle is that the fly — on a short leader of four to six feet — should fish at the level to which it is taken by the line, and not deeper (See Fig. 4). Submerged boulders and sudden changes in the depth of the water cause either some strong, bulging turbulence, or an acceleration in the speed of the current, and this pressure is able to hold the line and fly safely away from most sources of possible trouble. Hence the fly can be made to cover the adjacent lies effectively and with no loss of time.

Of course, the character of such pools is that the average depth is much less than that of the long stretches of smoother, steady flow that suit spinning so well. And for sunk-line fishing to be really enjoyable, the water should not be over-deep. The nicest fishing is when the depth does not exceed about six or seven feet, but a short stretch of deeper water can be searched quite pleasurably with the fly. When the deeper water is rather extensive, however, it is not interesting for sunk-line fishing.

In normal seasons there are long periods when the water temperature is between the lower and upper forties. The rather shallower and often rougher pools are then well populated. And when in the taking mood, the salmon are more easily deceived by a rather smaller lure that approaches at two feet or more above the bottom. Then the 2in. to 2½in. Devon can be fished downstream and across on the heavy spinning tackle without undue trouble in the way of getting snagged. And it may be thought to be a true alternative to sunk-line fishing. But many anglers believe that when the water is clear, the more natural and variable way in which the fly moves in the current is decidedly more effective than the more regular behaviour of the relatively heavier spinning lures.

The popular practice is to favour the fly when the water is clear and the speed of the flow is not too fast to allow the line to come round reasonably steadily. And when the water is rather high or coloured, spinning is acknowledged to have the advantage.

II. Flies for orthodox sunk-line fishing

Today the old types of single and double irons are very rarely used. For fishing the stronger flows, the patented trebles with long shanks, either rigid or articulate, and aluminium tube-flies behave very satisfactorily. For the more gentle current, the plastic tube-fly is extremely suitable. A short piece of rubber, or very pliable plastic tube that fits over the eye of the treble and the end of the body tube, is useful to keep the hook in the correct position and still allow it the necessary freedom of movement when a salmon is being played. Some anglers are distrustful of the long, rigid shanks because of the possibility of their acting as levers against the hook-holds.

III. Rods, reels and lines

The rod should be capable of throwing a long line with both

the overhead and the various kinds of roll cast. Thirteen to fourteen feet is the most suitable, and since modern salmon rods are so pleasingly light, there is seldom any reason why the angler should have to compromise on this question. There is sometimes a tendency to think in terms of big rods for big rivers and small rods for small rivers, but as will be seen shortly, the length of the rod is very important from the tactical point of view. It should not be thought that because a shorter one will throw the line as far as may be required, it will also perform all the other duties to full satisfaction.

As for the reel, consistent with plenty of capacity to hold the bulky line plus about one hundred yards of strong backing, it should be as light as possible. An exposed rim for braking when playing fish is a very desirable feature, but care must be taken to avoid damage to the rim and the intrusion of sand beneath it, either of which can cause the reel to lock.

Double-taper, oil-dressed silk lines have proved their worth over the years in orthodox sunk-line fishing and as yet, they have not by any means been superceded. The plastic-coated, slow-sinking line is delightful for casting and performs beautifully in the stronger flows where its ability to penetrate more readily and thus fish the fly deeper and/or more slowly is an advantage. But it does not hold its position in the steadier currents as well as silk, and then it cannot be made to fish as slowly. Since it is never wise, however, on a visit to the river for any kind of fishing to depend entirely on one reel which may go wrong, it is a good plan to have an oil-dressed silk line – a no. 6 or perhaps a no. 5 – on one reel and an AFTM 8, 9, or 10 plastic-coated slow-sinker on the other.

IV. Tactics

First it must be decided how the rod should be held. Some years ago there was a fashion to keep the tip close to the surface of the water and pointing in the same direction as the line. The idea was that when an offer came, a big coil of line could be released by the left hand, thus avoiding any undue resistance being felt by the fish. Many anglers found, however, that they did not always succeed in letting the line go before first feeling a heavy tug on the rod, and then the incident came to nothing. In any case, though, this method is very restrictive in several important respects and is also a comparatively uncomfortable and fatiguing way to hold the rod.

When the rod is held at an angle of about fortyfive degrees with the button resting against the thigh, and the shoulders held back, the strain is quite negligible. And if the rod is pointed squarely across the current after the cast has been made and the tip swung slowly round as the line fishes across the current, it causes less pull on the line than when the tip is kept low. This makes an appreciable difference in reducing the drag on the fly when that is wished.

Superficially it may seem that the rod held at a low angle would assist the line to fish deeper, but this is not so, because the tip supports the line too much where it enters the water and helps the pressure of the flow from underneath to push the line upwards. But when curving down from the tip of the rod held higher, the weight of the line is not supported at the

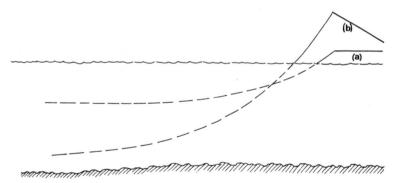

With the rod held low (a) the line is supported where it enters the water; with the rod high (b) the line fishes deeper

FIG. 5

point where it enters the water (See Fig. 5). And the swinging round of the rod through the bigger arc helps to reduce rather than increase the upward pressure of the current, because the point of entry moves downstream as it comes round.

Perhaps more important than these undoubted advantages, however, is the fact that when an offer comes with the rod held fairly high, the tightening of the line gives one plenty of warning to drop the rod point before the fish feels any strain, and this produces some slack line more rapidly and with less resistance than can be achieved in any other way. But before dealing with the procedure for hooking the fish, other line-controlling techniques must be mentioned.

As a general rule, the longer the line thrown, the deeper and slower it will fish. And apart from a little care in getting the angle of the cast right in the first place – a bigger angle downstream in faster water as in heavy spinning – the fly will fish round entirely satisfactorily without any further help in much of the water that is fished.

There are frequent occasions, of course, when action must be taken in faster currents to slow the speed of the fly down and make it fish deeper. With this in view, it is popular practice when wading or fishing from a suitable bank, to make the new cast before taking the customary two or three paces downstream to the point from which the fly will be fished round. This does help the line to go down further in a convenient manner, and when coupled with a long throw, it may be all that is necessary.

A standard drill when fishing the faster flows is to make a large upstream mend as soon as the fly touches the water. This is very effective in helping the line to sink and in slowing down its pace in crossing the current. This technique is sufficiently important to warrant close examination; and the explanation makes it possible to appreciate at the one time both the means of removing or reducing the influences that make the line move round too quickly, and fail to sink sufficiently.

If the mend is not made, the line lies across the current at an angle of, say, forty degrees. And since the rod is retarding the line, the current is able to exert a great deal of side pressure against it. This pushes the line quickly through a reducing angle towards full conformity with the direction of the flow; and in doing so, while the line is held back by the rod, the pressure of the current beneath the line is caused to build up. Hence the fly swings round too quickly and at too shallow a depth.

The upstream mend, however, lays the line at a new angle more closely in line with the flow, thus reducing the amount of side pressure to which it is subjected. Also, the mend puts a big curve into the line near to the rod (See Fig. 6). This drifts downstream as it straightens out and in effect, it is equivalent to feeding a length of slack at a controlled rate. Thus the line is retarded much less and therefore the pressure beneath the line is reduced. Now, there being a reduction in pressure in both dimensions, the line moves more slowly across the current and sinks faster. In the short space of time

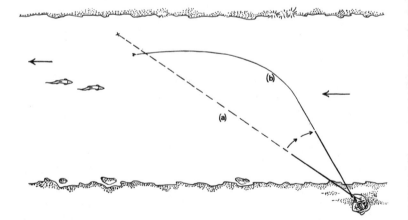

FIG. 6

required for the line to be straightened as much as will occur, the fly reaches the required position and will proceed to fish across the lie at the speed and depth wished.

It will now be seen why there was no recommendation of the shooting head and monofilament backing for this type of fishing. If a long line were thrown, which is, of course, the purpose of the shooting head, the mend would have to be made largely with the monofilament, and this lacks the weight to transmit the necessary movement to the fly line. The monofilament actually assists the sinking of the shooting head, but this is of no help when the angle at which is crosses the flow cannot be altered by the mend.

Although this question of the speed and depth at which the fly fishes never ceases to be of primary tactical importance, the amount of latitude becomes considerably greater after the water temperature has risen the crucial small amount that makes the smaller sizes of sunk flies fished further from the bottom the most suitable. Then three most helpful changes take effect. It is far less difficult to ensure that the salmon will not fail to see the lure, partly due to the higher angle of sight and also because the fish are more alert. Secondly the salmon show more willingness to move variable distances either straight ahead, or at a tangent, and upwards, to meet the fly. And lastly, what is perhaps the most important is that once the fish has started the move towards the lure, it will rarely fail to make a successful interception although the target may not maintain such a regular course as the heavier lure used in spinning. This lively action of the lightweight lure in the turbulence of the current is probably one of the principal reasons why it is so successful with the autumn-run salmon.

V. Hooking the salmon

The old idea that the salmon should be given plenty of time after taking the large fly is certainly well founded, and no-one would dispute that the best hook-hold can be expected to result when the leader is in a position down-stream of the fish. But the provision of many yards of slack, so that the line will drift down a long way past the salmon, and the prolonged delay,which are sometimes recommended, seem to be a big exaggeration of the needs. When fishing from a suitable bank, or if the wading is safe and easy, it is undoubtedly helpful to heed the popular view that one should take two or three paces downstream as the first reaction to the offer — before the fish has felt the resistance of the rod, of course — but even this is by no means essential. With the rod held reasonably high when the line is seen to be tightening, it is enough to lower the rod instantly and release a yard or so of slack line from the left hand. A few seconds later, the strain will gradually be felt to build up and then as the rod begins to respond, very firm pressure should be applied until the fish sets off to commence the fight. This convenient and straight forward system is very reliable.

SUPER-HEAVY SUNK-LINE FISHING

The class of water where mandatory fly fishing takes the place of heavy spinning is usually too deep to permit any wading. And fishing from the bank with the sunk line in very deep water is far too laborious and unpromising to be interesting. The use of the super-heavy tackle is, therefore, almost entirely restricted to fishing from boats. This means that although the angler casts and attempts to control the line, it is the way in which the boat is handled that finally decides whether the presentation of the fly is slow enough and sufficiently close to the bottom to be effective.

Gillies require to be knowledgeable and enthusiastic enough cheerfully to persevere with the exacting, hard work. Most of them are, of course, very capable and also willing, although their role in organizing the final, telling part of the behaviour of the lure may tend to be underestimated. This is not said to pay gratuitous compliments to gillies, but to show that there must be co-operation and agreement between the hands on the rod and those on the oars.

Stage one of the super-heavy fishing is to use the normal sunk-line rod with a fast-sinking synthetic line and normal sunk flies, but also including tube-flies dressed on copper tubing as well as those on lighter materials. This outfit may be very suitable for occasions when the river is at normal level or lower and the pools are not excessively deep. However, the management of the fast-sinking line between fishing one cast out and making the next throw is a slow affair requiring a lot of care. Big draws of line must be retrieved and laid in the bottom of the boat before the line remaining in the water is sufficiently close to the surface to permit a reasonably clean back-cast. Then some false casting and line lengthening is usually necessary before there is the right balance for making the next long throw.

On some of the smaller fly-only rivers, the fast sinker is used as a substitute for the spinning tackle when the water is high and running very fast. It can be quite successful and not at all unpleasant, but it is certainly not as efficient as spinning in those circumstances. And when the fly rod does become the most effective, it is not the fast sinker that is used.

An alternative way of using the normal sunk-line rod for the first stage of super-heavy fishing in the least difficult conditions is to put a spiral lead on the slow sinker or silk line, close to the connection with the leader. Of course, this makes the casting very ugly and potentially dangerous, but it will get the lure down to the big depths when the flow is fairly gentle.

For stage two, a very powerful rod is essential and for the best results it should be no shorter than about fifteen feet. Fortunately the modern versions are remarkably light compared with their predecessors, and the fishing can be much more pleasant than it was just a few years ago. Nevertheless, well-accustomed muscles remain at a premium.

The heaviest fast-sinker — the AFTM no. 12 — is wanted to give the maximum scope to deal with the deep, heavy flows, and this often requires to be aided by extra weight in the fly — lead wire wrapped round the copper tube-fly. Normal fly-rods will not deal with such a load, certainly not without putting the angler at serious risk of injury by the fly. But providing there is no attempt to make false casts with too much line, the powerful fifteen-footer should keep the heavy fly moving high enough in the air for reasonable safety. Nevertheless, when the angler is cold and fatigued, he should remember what a lethal missile the heavy fly can be. If the boatman starts hunching up, it is usually a sincere and wise intimation that the time has come for a break.

The heavy shooting-head and monofilament backing are very suitable for this type of fishing. Very long distances can be thrown and the temptation to lift and aerialize too much line is removed. The backing must be retrieved and dropped at the feet as a matter of course until the rear end of the shooting-head is within a yard of the rod tip. Then everything is automatically right for lifting the line in preparation for the next cast. Also the shooting-head makes a useful reduction in the amount of false casting which may be needed.

Very little scope is available for variations in the control of the line. Mending is out of the question and it cannot be hoped to fish the lure through a big arc unless there is a good deal of lateral movement by the boat, which is a difficult manoeuvre in the fast flow where it is most wanted.

There are plenty of situations, of course, that do not present the maximum difficulties and many a day can be thoroughly enjoyable in every respect. But the limitations of a method of fishing must be recognized and acknowledged if the angler is to see his opportunities in the way that will enable him to make the most of them.

When the level of the water is rather high and it is difficult to find casts where the fly will move round sufficiently slowly, a strong flow that runs at a fairly big tangent away from the bank often creates the only favourable fishing area. It is usually not too difficult for the gillie to hold the boat between the bank and the edge of the strong current, and, of course, the best lies are likely to be in the steadier flow alongside the strong current. Due to the angle of the flow, however, the fly moves round at a relatively slow speed even in the fastest water and this makes it easy to cover the lies just as steadily as may be wished. It is often possible in such places to fish successfully with a comparatively short line, and this alone is a worthwhile consideration when the river generally presents the maximum difficulties.

Needless to say, with a lot of heavy line deeply submerged, the scope for action when an offer comes is very restricted. Although the pull from the fish can feel very heavy — since it works with the current and not against it — even a very forceful movement of the rod would probably only succeed in bending it and hardly produce a nudge at the fly. Also it is unlikely to be any use giving line, because the fish is nearly certain to have felt a lot of resistance before that could become effective. There is little option, therefore, than to hold very firmly against the tightening of the line when an offer is detected. No doubt due to the slowness of the reactions of the salmon in those circumstances, however, the proportion of the offers that is successfully dealt with is usually quite satisfactory. The probability is, of course, that most of the fish hook themselves against the resistance of the heavy line, more or less regardless of any action which the angler may take.

4 The Floating Line and Subsurface Fly

I. Progress or retrogression?

The question may seem rather academic at the moment in view of the sad state of the salmon stocks during the past three or four years, but the seasoned angler must have doubts about the current trend in fishing the floating line.

Adequate coverage of the water is undoubtedly easier with modern equipment than ever before. No advice on casting will be offered here because that subject is better left to the specialists who understand the most successful teaching techniques. But the coaching required to correct the principal faults now brings about such impressive improvements that learning has been made far less troublesome. And any failure to catch fish these days can rarely be blamed on the casting, as it so often could be in the past. No doubt the presence of UDN can make the salmon most unwilling to rise to the subsurface fly: nevertheless, there would appear to be grounds for suspecting that this is not the only trouble.

Many anglers are either prepared to accept the statement of some manufacturers that the tendency of the tip of the floating line to sink beneath the surface is exactly what is wanted to present the subsurface fly correctly, or they do not consider the matter to be of any particular importance. Also they show little concern about the length of the nylon leader: they do not mind variations of two or three feet so long as it does not look too short. And they cheerfully change about from metal-shanked flies to those dressed on very light tubes with seemingly no interest in the question of the relative weights. Clearly their attitude is that if the fly is somewhere in the vicinity of the surface of the water, that is good enough. But is it?

In the times of the earlier famous names connected with *greased-line* fishing, there were certainly great debates about the right and wrong ways of presenting the fly. One angler with a really formidable record of salmon caught would be said to have had the wrong idea by another whose success, though admirable, was no better. Yet another would have a different view again, which he could support with seemingly convincing data.

As time went along, the different styles advocated each won their converts, and the arguments continued. But the motives of some of the more recent debaters have been suspect, because the plain truth of the position was established years ago. All the one-time controversial methods concerning the placing of the line and the way in which it should be mended, left unchecked, or guided round, which have appeared in the highly-regarded books, plus numerous examples that have not been given the same amount of publicity, have each been recognized to be correct according to the circumstances.

It seems that the original difficulties arose from the fact that most of the more famous contentions were based on the results achieved in one particular class of water at the special time of the year when it was most heavily populated by reasonably fresh-run salmon. Elsewhere in pools of very different character and with fish belonging to earlier or later runs, the successful techniques were naturally different. Had the various factions joined forces and reached agreement on an overall, progressive policy, it would have saved a lot of the subsequent, futile argument.

The effectual revelations from this snippet of history, however, are of the utmost significance. All the anglers concerned fished with the oil-dressed silk-line — there was no other — which was greased to make it float. Once the tip of the line began to sink, which often happened, the whole of it soon started to go under to a big depth and made fishing impossible. The result was that everyone was very line conscious. The moment the tip started behaving suspiciously, it was dried most carefully and regreased. The line had to float perfectly no matter how much time was lost in ensuring this.

Leaders in those days were silk-worm gut *casts*. Making them up from the short strands of the suitable strength was a skilled professional job and they were costly items. The standard length for greased-line fishing was nine feet and this was universally accepted. Of course, the gut had to be soaked in water thoroughly before it was used, and then it held its position in the flow without the trouble sometimes experienced with nylon: but again this was a common factor for all concerned. And another common factor was that most anglers used only the Low Water hooks — mostly singles, but a few did favour doubles.

Thus it will be seen that the only scope for variation in the way a fly was presented was in the speed at which it was fished. The angle of the cast and mending were virtually the only basic differences that could be made. And whether the anglers were very conscious of the fact or not — though there is very little doubt that they were — the depth at which the fly was fished was automatically controlled very strictly indeed by all of them.

With this understanding of the tackle used and the concise descriptions available of the techniques employed, it is quite clear that in all true greased-lining conditions, the smallest sizes of fly were fished just fractionally beneath the surface, and the largest only a matter of three or four inches down. And to repeat, the various techniques that followed this principle produced catches which proved beyond doubt that the relative presentation of the fly was very acceptable indeed to the salmon.

One of the basic tenets which will be observed in this chapter, therefore, is that the depth at which the subsurface fly is fished is a crucial factor.

II. Strategy

It will not now require to be stated that the success in the early season of the large and rather formless sunk fly is no reflection on the vision of the salmon. And when its good sight is matched by the state of mental alertness that results in response to the very small illusion near the surface of the water in a turbulent flow, one can be certain that nothing which could present possible danger to the fish will escape notice. Perhaps the image of the angler moving along the bank will not scare the salmon into panicky flight, but that cannot be interpreted to mean that there is genuine indifference. It may be instinctive for the salmon to rely on natural camouflage within certain limits, and there is no doubt that many fish do escape notice entirely. In any case, however, it is easy enough in practice to prove that any preoccupation by the fish which may result from the angler's lack of care concerning concealment is at the cost of its interest in the fly.

It is no exaggeration to say that the bank discipline of the spring and summer salmon angler should be just as strict as that of the dry-fly fisher for trout on a chalkstream. The cover provided when wading in rough, fast water is, of course, very good and presents no problem providing the approach has been suitably careful. But in smoother flows, particularly when there has been any risk of being seen on the skyline, any sudden appearance or fast movement can ruin chances of sport in the pool for some considerable time.

Some reasonably successful anglers have little or no faith in the sporting potential of smooth water, irrespective of its speed. This attitude is very restrictive on many good pools and is, no doubt, due in part to lack of bank discipline. Another point of equal importance, however, is often involved. Observations kept on a salmon when an angler has been working his way down a pool — both fishing skilfully and paying all due regard to the need for concealment — have shown that the fish becomes aware of what is occurring on and near the surface of the water when the fly is as much as twenty yards beyond taking range. For some time previously the fish would maintain a constant poise and rate of movement, if any, of the tail and fins. But eventually, another cast that brought the fly yet a little closer would cause a sudden change in the fish. First the salmon would seem to stiffen momentarily, and then resume its movements, but at a noticeably more rapid rate. If within not more than two or three casts later, the fly crossed the river within taking range, the fish probably rose and took without hesitation. But when the angler moved down the pool too slowly and made numerous further casts after the signal of recognition, and before presenting the fly within range, the fish then ignored it almost invariably. Clearly too many sightings of the fly out of range have the effect of detracting from the responsive urge by the time it is within easy reach.

Obviously this is a question of degree which must be judged by the angler in each different situation. The ruling circumstances will alter the spacing that should be made between casts, but the overall policy should undoubtedly be to ensure that the fish should never be allowed to see the fly more than two or three times at the most before it is within comfortable taking range. This may mean having to take as many as ten or more paces between casts on occasions. And when that is necessary, one can be sure that denser coverage would put the fish off for some considerable time. But providing the pool is long enough to require fifteen or twenty minutes to cover it at this fast rate, the big spacing will usually mean that it will stand up to being fished down again straight afterwards.

A good appreciation of this need to avoid overfishing the water is also a good guide to the needs in faster, more turbulent currents. It is rarely any advantage to cast more than once and fish the fly round in the same way from any one point. There is little risk of the fish failing to see the fly if a minimum spacing of three paces between casts is always maintained. That should ensure that the second or third time down the pool will be just as promising as the first. Indeed, familiarity with some pools shows that they have a tendency to fish better the second or third time down than the first. One could imagine that in some lies – possibly a little deeper than average – after the salmon has seen the fly go by once without feeling a strong enough urge to rise and take it, the second sighting following a suitable delay is less resistible. This can mean that one rod following another at a short interval may get the offer, but there does seem to be the necessity for some delay even if it is only a few minutes.

III. Types of flies

At water temperatures below $48^{\circ}F$ when it is wished to fish the fly much deeper than in the orthodox floating-line style, aluminium tube-flies and the two kinds of long-shanked trebles are very effective. They are also useful for fishing near the surface in the stronger flows so long as the size required is no less than about one inch. When the water temperature climbs into the fifties, however, and the smaller sizes are wanted, the Low Water and standard singles and doubles, and the plastic tube-flies are more suitable for fishing at the appropriate depth.

Tube-flies will not, of course, produce images as slender as those on the metal shanks. Hence there would seem to be some advantage in using tubes when the silhouette patterns are wanted in very strong light, and also when a bigger impact seems necessary with the normal image/silhouette in a coloured water. But the more slender bodies of the Low

Water flies are generally thought to be preferable for the translucent illusion and normal image, while the weights of the Low Water and standard irons are better suited to most of the occasions when the flashing illusion patterns are wanted. (This shows a useful, subsidiary reason for knowing fly patterns by groupings.)

In comparable sizes, the Low Water hooks tend to fish slightly deeper than plastic tubes and the tactical position should be considered when any interchanging is done. It should also be mentioned, though, that flies dressed on very small lead tubes are the best of all for avoiding skimming in fast glides with small flies.

From the physical point of view, Low Water singles are the best for casting and the most trouble-free. Doubles sometimes get reversed on the leader and plastic tubes are very prone to this fault. When the wind is at all difficult, the single iron has a great advantage over all other types.

The most important consideration of all as far as types of flies are concerned, however, is the need for a progressive basis of judgment for controlling the depth at which the lure fishes. Due to the increased water resistance caused by the extra bulk of the tube-fly, the larger sizes do not necessarily fish deeper than the smaller ones and one cannot be sure of making the changes which are practically automatic with single irons. The simplest solution, of course, is to fish singles at all times, but plans can include other types to advantage when their particular characteristics are not opposed to the requirements of the occasion. For example, when the smallish lure requires to be very near the surface in popply water, the plastic tube can hardly fail to perform correctly. In a glide, however, it would be very difficult to prevent the same fly from skimming.

IV. Rods and reels

Provided sufficient care is taken with the selection, the modern rod used for orthodox sunk-line fishing should be perfectly suitable for all floating-line work when a double-handed rod is required. The same versatility in casting and line-controlling ability are needed: therefore the good length of thirteen to fourteen feet remains equally desirable. When the water is very low in summer and an extra-fine leader is used, a single-handed rod of 9ft 6in. to 10ft 6 in. will often do everything that is required and then, being more gentle, it is preferable to the big rod.

The reel requires to have fully as much capacity as for sunk-line fishing. And since finer leaders are used, the smooth braking made possible by the exposed rim makes this type even more desirable for fishing the floating line.

V. Lines

This is a very complex question. Several may be needed and since convenience demands that each should have its own reel, one naturally wishes to make sure of getting the best results for the considerable outlay.

Double-taper lines are essential when any kind of roll casting is required, and are therefore the most generally useful. At the same time, when the water is clear and the salmon may be rather sensitive, most anglers will only resort to Spey casts and switches if the situation will not permit the use of the overhead cast. And although the plastic-coated double-taper floaters shoot beautifully and make long, overhead casting comparatively easy, the individual must decide whether he can afford always to be without a forward-taper line. Besides the way in which this variety assists in achieving long distances effortlessly and without an unduly long back-cast, the particular construction is very helpful where there is slack water, or a very strong current, between the rod and the flow which it is wished to fish. The fine section behind the forward taper can often be held clear of the water without adversely affecting the way the heavier, water-borne part of the line behaves. On many beats this ability to cope effectively with unhelpful water that has to be bridged by the line is a vital matter.

The inherent fault of lines which are sufficiently buoyant to support themselves on the surface is, naturally, that the diameter is larger than one often wishes. This seldom causes much concern while the larger subsurface flies are in use. but it can be very important when the water is warmer and the salmon are more easily disturbed. Then one must consider the advantages of the fine oil-dressed silk line, which has a relatively good casting potential for its appreciably smaller cross-section. Casting instructors are naturally very keen that their pupils should use lines that develop the action of their rods sufficiently to make the casting as effortless as possible. But good modern salmon rods will throw much lighter lines satisfactorily than the precise sizes they were designed to carry in order to give maximum performance. And if it becomes necessary to use a finer line to catch fish, one should certainly not be hidebound by the idea that the rod must always be perfectly balanced by the line. No. 3 oil-dressed silk lines caught enormous numbers of salmon on thirteen and fourteen footers long before the modern, very much lighter and more versatile rods were introduced.

Some thought must also be given to the question of the colour of the line. The ease with which the white floater can be seen on the water in most lights is quite delightful and it would be a pity to miss this advantage in the spring when the river is in good form and the salmon not too sensitive. But all the claims about the white line being less visible to the fish cannot be accepted at face value. Against the bright background of the sky, the silhouette only must be seen, while at a lower angle of sight where the background is likely to be the reflection of the bed of the river on the under-surface of the water, the white may be a very obvious contrast. Also in bright conditions the white flashes a lot in the air. Dry-fly fishers for trout have had many experiences of putting the fish down before the fly touched the water;

Above top: The Tweed at Upper Hendersyde. A famous spring fishery, for either fly or bait.

Above: The Lune at Newton. An ever-changing pool due to shingle movements.

Above top: The Eden at Kirkoswald. A fascinating pool made very complex by deep pots and submerged rocks.

Above: The Nith near Thornhill. A very high, coloured water.

but on changing to a dark-coloured line, they caught fish immediately. It is also well to remember that the greens and browns of the oil-dressed silk lines served wonderfully well before the introduction of the white lines. There are certainly many very experienced salmon fishers who are quite convinced that it is a mistake to use a white line when the water is low and clear.

Every choice of line is more or less a compromise; therefore the first decision to be made in each case is whether priority should be given to physical considerations, or the need to cause as little possible distraction to the fish as can be arranged. On this basis, the usual selection for much of the spring fishing will be a white, double-taper floater capable of reaching maximum distances, say an AFTM no. 9 or 10. As a supporting line for rather more difficult conditions concerning the fish themselves and for special situations regarding casting or line control, a green or brown forward-taper floater, say AFTM no. 7 or 8, could often be very useful. Then for the low waters in high summer, the finest oil-dressed silk line that can be managed reasonably well on both the single and double-handed rods – preferably a no. 3, but certainly no heavier than a no. 4 – would complete the requirements.

The double-taper floater incorporating a sinking tip can be very useful during the transitional period when it may be wished to get the fly down relatively very deep, and it would also have some uses later in heavy flows and strong glides; but ideally it should be additional to the three previously selected and not a substitute for any one of them.

If the reader accepts that good control of the depth at which the fly fishes is essential, he will agree that at least the first three or four yards of the synthetic floater should be treated with a silicone grease to ensure that it always rides high on the surface of the water. Manufacturers say that no grease should be applied, but the silicone variety does not appear to cause any more rapid deterioration than occurs when the line is left untreated.

It has become rather a common practice to join a collar of heavy gauge nylon by whipping or a nail-knot to the plastic-coated floater. This has a strong tendency to make the tip of the line sink. A much more simple and trouble-free method is to strip the dressing from the last inch of the core of the line, and join this to the loop of the leader with a figure-of-eight knot. If this inch of the core is kept saturated with silicone grease, it is a big help in keeping the tip of the line well up on the surface.

VI. Leaders

No doubt it will be agreed that it is a good plan to decide a standard length of the leader for all fishing with the floating line. There are obvious advantages in having as great a length as possible between the fly and the line, consistent with maintaining the capability to fish the smallest sizes of lure very close to the surface of the water. Twelve feet is very convenient in all respects.

With modern, high-grade monofilament, there is little to be gained by making up the leader in graduated strengths. Most anglers find a single length of one diameter entirely suitable. 11 lb test has all the strength needed for the heavier work with the larger flies. For normal conditions with the medium sized and small flies, 9 lb test is very suitable, while 7 lb test is usually as fine as one needs to go in low water conditions.

In order to remove any grease and ensure consistent, non-floating behaviour by the leader, it should always be rubbed down with a solution of fuller's earth and water before starting to fish, and whenever the leader has become dry between pools and so on. The mixture should have the consistency of cream. It can be used liberally and the current washes it off readily. The difference it makes, however, in getting the nylon to behave reliably well cannot be stressed too much.

VII. Mending the line

Some skilled anglers do their mending by sharp twitches of the rod tip which send ripples snaking down the line to the point where the correction is required. With respect it must be suggested that this makes mending unnecessarily difficult; and it may be the reason why it is sometimes said that one cannot mend with a forward-taper line.

A much more simple and controllable method is to make a smooth, unhurried, bowling movement with the rod tip. Assuming that the rod is being held by the right hand with the button resting against the thigh, the operation is carried out quite effortlessly by the one hand without changing the position of the rod button. Then, when wished, some slack can be released by the left hand and thrown into the mend. Naturally, when the mend is made immediately following the cast, both hands are employed.

With this method, one watches the line lifting and moving over in the direction wanted, and it can be checked at any point by lowering the rod. With the forward taper line, a little more power must be put into the movement of the finer rear portion to make it lift the heavier line ahead, but after a little practice there is unlikely to be the slightest difficulty.

VIII. Tactics

The perfect cast for fishing the subsurface fly is where the current gets evenly and progressively faster from the position of the rod to beyond the point where the fly will fall. Such circumstances often apply when fishing from a gradually shelving beach on the inside of a big, smooth bend in the river. There one can find the optimum angle of cast that will fish the fly all the way round exactly as wished and without the need for any mending. At the lower water temperatures for the subsurface fly, the longest line possible would be thrown at about sixty degrees. The arc traversed by the lure would then be fairly square across the current. And if its speed of movement were judged to be such as to give a salmon just enough time to rise and intercept it without delay, it would be considered suitable for a spell of trial fishing (see Fig. 7). On the other hand, the movement may appear to be too slow both to get the best response from the fish and to cover the water fast enough to search the pool without undue delay. In that case, the line should be shortened a little and thrown at a slightly less angle, say fifty degrees. Now the fly will cover the same distance, but in a shorter time, thus increasing the speed a little. A shorter line again at forty degrees would once more cover the same distance, but in a still shorter time, and therefore at an even greater speed.

If the first trial cast proved suitable to catch fish, say on a Low Water no. 4 fly, the second and third casts would be the kind of amendments probably required at higher temperatures to suit the no. 6 and no. 8 flies respectively.

When a narrow band of rather faster flow is crossed, it is easy to see how this pushes the line downstream at that point and drags the tip of the line and the fly across the water more

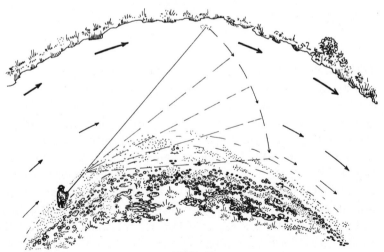

FIG. 7

quickly than was intended: hence the need for a mend to be made. Soon these requirements for corrections to be made in the lie of the line bring automatic reaction from the angler and present no problem. But one difficulty remains and it is the cause of the most common fault in fishing the floating line. The line on the surface is able to move much more freely than the fly working through the water. And if the flow, although not widly irregular, is such that a fairly pronounced concave bend develops in the line (see Fig. 8) one can be sure that the fly is dragging considerably more than might be suspected. In a gentle to moderate flow, this amount of drag may be just right to produce the correct movement of the fly, but in a faster current, it will usually be quite excessive.

This point must be watched particularly carefully when the fly is at the far side of a fast flow. The normal drill to compensate for this is to make the cast at a bigger angle downstream, but this alone is not enough in most cases and if corrective action is not taken, the fly will probably be left

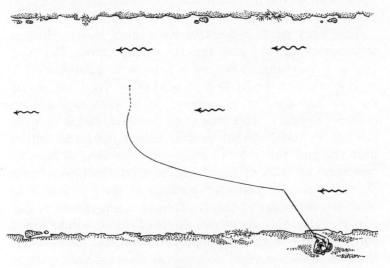

FIG. 8

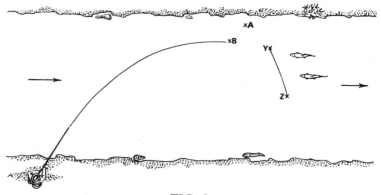

FIG. 9

upstream of the tip of the line and then it will shortly sweep round quite ridiculously. And, of course, once the excessive drag of the fly has started, it will not correct itself unaided while the cast is being fished out although it may soon go into an area of more steady flow. The big upstream mend right down to the tip of the line is essential to put an end to the excessive dragging.

This leads on to a point of line-control policy which is rarely practised, but is of the utmost importance. Referring to Fig. 9, most anglers wishing to fish the fly across the arc Y to Z would cast the fly to Y straight away. Then they would do any mending in accordance with what appeared to become necessary. This procedure, however, means that the fly has to travel a yard or two before the leader settles properly and the fly can fish well. But then it may be necessary to make a mend and another short spell must elapse before the corrected position of the line is able to affect the behaviour of the fly. Thus so much ground is lost that probably only about two-thirds of the arc will be fished correctly. Also there is the important point that the falling of the line onto the water so close to the position in which it is hoped that the fly will start fishing may easily distract the salmon.

A more suitable system is to make the cast so that the fly falls at point A, two or three yards upstream of the arc intended to be fished, and a yard or two further across the current. As soon as the fly touches the water, a large upstream mend is made which reaches right down to the fly, draws it to point B, and then leaves the line lying on the water with the lower portion parallel to the flow. Now, as was mentioned in connection with the large sunk-line mend, the angle at which the line closer to the rod crosses the current results in the fly making a controlled approach to the point Y where it is intended to start fishing. And there has been no disturbing splash at close quarters.

After the first such operation, one will know whether the original mend put into the line was sufficient to make the fly fish correctly from point Y. If necessary, a second mend can be made a little in advance of the fly reaching its fishing position, but this time, of course, it will be restricted to the line and should not draw the fly. From then on, further mends will be made whenever the movement of any part of the line on the water appears to be a potential threat to the intended behaviour of the fly.

A small extension to the procedure just described produces an invaluable manoeuvre for covering big areas of suitable flow which are situated on the far side of a powerful current. When the cast is made, a loop of several yards of slack is held by the left hand. After the big upstream mend has been made, the line is mended again immediately, but only as far as the edge of the steadier flow; and at the same time the slack is released, thus placing several yards of the line nearest to the rod across the strongest part of the current at a very acute angle. Being almost parallel with the flow, this upper part of the line only moves across very slowly, and only exerts a gentle pull on the big shoulder crossing the steadier flow. Fig. 10 shows the position after the first, big mend, and Fig. 11 shortly after the second, smaller mend. It will be

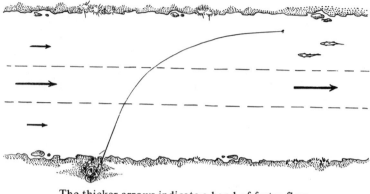

The thicker arrows indicate a band of faster flow.
FIG. 10

appreciated that the upper portion of the line performs the rôle of a slowly moving hinge, which allows the shoulder to straighten out smoothly. Hence the fly drops gently downstream and across, covering the lies at a suitable speed. There must be no delay in making the second mend, and, of course, all parts of the line drift with the current quickly until the line is fairly tight between the rod and the start of the big shoulder, which means that the fly does not start fishing

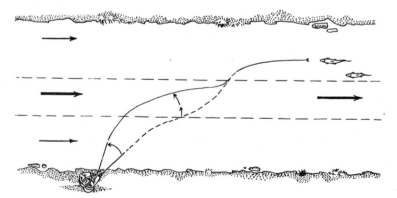

FIG. 11

correctly until that stage has been reached. Therefore plenty of space must be allowed between the rod and the lies to be covered to ensure that the first fishing track of the fly will be at a suitable distance upstream of the fish.

The ability to perform this manoeuvre increases the angler's effective scope enormously. Once it has been mastered, there are very few problems in dealing with the current that present any insuperable difficulties.

Less experienced anglers may think that paying so much attention to the question of mending is unnecessarily finicky, but when the difference can be observed from a point of vantage between a fly fishing correctly and one being dragged round out of control, all doubt is quickly removed. At the same time, it must be agreed that too much mending that causes the fly to fish more slowly than the occasion requires is just as much a fault as allowing the leader to drag the fly round too quickly.

Downstream mends are occasionally worth trying, but this method of *leading* the fly is most commonly used in situations where another technique would probably be better. Before going any further, however, one must decide what action of the fly is normally the most desirable in a suitably favourable flow. The most popular and generally profitable method of fishing across the current with the line controlled from a point well upstream causes the fly to be heading into the stream all the time: it gains a little here and loses a bit there according to the variations in the speed of the flow; but it loses ground overall and finishes up at a position relatively further downstream than where it started at the beginning of the arc. A little reflection will show that this is also the most common and successful behaviour of the heavy spinning lure and sunk-line fly. And one can imagine — whether or not it is really relevant — that a very small fish or nymph that had insufficient power to make headway against the current would end up behaving in exactly the same way as the fly fishing as just described. This can, therefore, be thought to be a natural movement and it is certainly very effective in exciting the reflexes of the salmon.

It has been recommended from time to time that when the fly has fished through a nice flow and then starts moving towards the side too slowly, a downstream mend should be thrown into the line so that the fly will be drawn across the steadier water more quickly. Perhaps this will prove successful on occasions, but it will be appreciated that it causes the fly to move head-first towards the side. In the majority of situations of this sort, however, an alternative technique is likely to be more effective. The rod tip will have followed the line round to the point where the fly begins to slow down too much. Then the rod should be swung round smoothly so that it points obliquely towards the bank and line should be coiled in the left hand. This keeps the fly moving towards the side, but also heading into the flow and possibly gaining on it to some extent. If the area of poor flow is too much to be handled by coiling line, the alternative is to make slow, smooth draws. When wading up to the knees or deeper, the fly may be taken by a salmon directly below the angler and only a few yards away. In such a case, it is usually the best plan to drop the rod point instantly and release the line from the left hand. If the fish then moves out into the current, as it probably will, the chance of a hook-hold in the corner of the mouth will be quite good.

The situation best suited to the downstream mend is where the flow all the way across is rather too weak to carry the fly correctly without assistance. For it to be the most effective, however, there requires to be sufficient breeze to ripple the surface. Here again, the track of the fly can be prolonged by handlining, or by *backing-up*. Normally, of course, the angler will only resort to this method when the better flows have become too shallow to offer the fish sufficient cover. At the same time, there are occasions in hot weather when the river is at normal level and the fish seek shelter in steady, deeper water, presumably from an excessive availability of oxygen.

Then the appearance of some heavy cloud and a relatively cool breeze may bring the fish onto the take in a remarkably short time. Should such a change in the overhead conditions prove to be fairly permanent, however, the activity of the fish will probably soon lead to the departure from the steadier water in favour of the runs again.

When the small summer salmon and grilse are about, the angler may wish to cast much more squarely and allow the fly to travel more downstream with the current as it gradually fishes its way to the side. Now the need to avoid splashing the line too near to the fish is more important than ever, but this presents no difficulty. After the fly has fished round from the one position, the next, squarish cast should be made before the angler takes up his new position. The moment the line has settled on the water, he should move down at the same speed as the line and then stop at the point, say after five paces, from which he will fish the cast out. While he is moving alongside the line, the fly is given the opportunity to sink a little deeper than may be wished, and therefore, when he stops, the rod should be lifted slightly to draw the line and bring the fly up to the correct level very near to the surface. After this, the pull of the line coming round on the surface will keep the fly moving at the correct speed and depth. Although so very simple, this drill is quite invaluable when the fish are at all shy.

The behaviour of the fly will probably take the form of alternating short intervals of heading into the flow and then towards the side, but always with a fairly lively movement both laterally and with the current. And this does seem to be more attractive to the small fish than the steadier, more consistent action which seems to be the best prior to the arrival of the summer runs.

Tactical consideration should also be given to the direction of any sunshine there might be, with particular attention to the question of shadow. When possible it is naturally better to cast towards the strong light than with one's back to it.

And providing conditions are favourable for the fish to be in a responsive humour, sunshine that is not at a bad angle is more help than hindrance. Indeed, dull daylight is un-doubtedly much the worst to have to contend with in the way of the vision of the salmon being too critical. But one particular point about the direction of the sunshine must be watched carefully. When the line lies on the water at a good big angle to the direction of the light rays, the shadow made is only of moderate intensity and is easily dispersed by the irregularities in the surface of the water and the current. Should the line point – in the horizontal plane – directly towards the sun, however, the shadow is very dense indeed. It is not an uncommon experience to see a salmon jump over the line and then repeat the performance each time the line crosses the same position. It will be found almost invariably when this happens that the line is, in fact, pointing directly towards the sun. Presumably the dense shadow looks like a wall of darkness approaching the fish, and as far as it is concerned, the jump is made to clear the wall and not over the line. Needless to say, the time when the fly is covering the lie must not coincide with that of the line lying directly towards the sun.

After a hot, sunny afternoon, the first sport likely to be had in the evening will probably be in the shade of tall trees. Details of the times when any such good casts first start to benefit from shade are well worth noting for future reference.

IX. Rises to the fly

If the line appears simply to halt before beginning to tighten as the result of an offer, or when the rise is seen on the surface to be in direct line with the flow, it is generally regarded as an indication that the presentation of the fly was within the correct bracket in all respects. On the other hand, a rather hurried-looking offer across the current – which usually occurs during the later stages of fishing the fly round – is thought to suggest that either the lure was crossing the flow too quickly, or had failed to make sufficient impact during the approach to the optimum position for interception by the fish.

It is always possible, of course, that in any individual lie the salmon may have been unsighted to the particular approach of the fly until it was too late for the fish to take in the most effortless manner. Therefore, too much should not be read into isolated cases of relatively clumsy takes out of line with the flow. It is not uncommon, however, for two or three such late offers to follow each other during a short spell of fishing; and then it must be suspected that there is something wrong with the presentation of the fly. Naturally this requires to be put right because in addition to reducing the chances of securing good hook-holds, it could mean that many more fish had seen the lure without feeling any urge to move to it.

It should be fairly obvious when it is the excessive speed of the lure that is at fault, and the mending necessary to rectify that should be no problem. (If the current is not too fast for the fish to be lying there, neither should it be too fast to control the line suitably). The next question then is whether the size or the pattern of the fly requires changing.

Clearly the image had failed to make the required impact soon enough. Therefore if the pattern concerned was of the silhouette type, the only course would be to increase the size. But had it been less dense, such as a Logie, either the pattern only could be changed, say to a Blue Charm of the same size; or a slightly larger Logie could be substituted. Either of those changes should make a small increase in the impact of the fly. But unless there appeared to be some very strong reason concerning the light which suggested that the change should definitely be made in the pattern, the normal preference would be to take advantage of the opportunity to use a slightly larger iron.

There is a fairly common tendency among anglers to

assume that if there appears to be anything wrong with the performance of the fly, the safest correction to make is always to substitute a smaller one. This may well be true when there are good indications that the salmon are in a favourable mood and no offer has been forthcoming. But whenever the fish make moves of any sort that result in close approaches to the fly without actually taking it, the remedy is far more likely to be found in the use of a larger size. The *short rise* in the gliding type of water is a common phenomenon, especially when the fish elsewhere are showing a preference for the lure to be not too close to the surface. For example, when a salmon has been taken in a lively current on a Low Water no. 6 Blue Charm, the same fly in a glide would be inclined to fish appreciably nearer to the surface and perhaps only attract a short rise. Then the same pattern on, say a no. 4 standard iron, fishing slightly deeper due to the greater weight, could be expected to result in a solid take.

The salmon rarely provide any clear demonstration of the fact – except in the purely negative way – when the fault with the fly is that it is rather too large and fishing too deeply. There is, however, one classical type of experience which can be taken as a sign that the lure should be smaller and kept nearer to the surface. Occasionally the only offers that come occur just at the moment when the line is being mended. Often it is then assumed that the correction to the line had reached right down to the fly and that the resultant twitch had attracted the salmon. This could hardly be so because at least a little lapse of time would be required for the fish to rise to the fly after seeing the twitch. It is much more probable that the salmon started to rise at the same time as the mending commenced. And since the mend would be thought necessary because there were indications of too much drag, the probability would be that the offer came because the fly had begun to fish faster and much nearer to the surface. The apparent solution – which has often been confirmed by experience – is that a slightly smaller size of the same pattern should be substitued, and this should be fished a little faster than was thought necessary in the first place. Automatically this would mean that the presentation would also be nearer to the surface.

When the small fly is fished very close to the surface, but is also travelling downstream rather quickly following a squarish cast, both salmon and grilse take with the precision of a trout collecting a spent spinner from the skin of the water. Their noses pop out just a fraction above the surface while the flies are being scooped in. Clearly the fish judge the location of the lure relative to the surface with absolute accuracy and are in no way deceived in that respect. And it would seem that this close proximity to the surface is often an essential factor in fishing the smaller lures.

As soon as grilse and small summer salmon are mentioned in this present context, the point must be made that there should be no confusion between fish *rising short* and *taking short*. If the fish seizes the lure, though only for a very brief spell, there can be no criticism of the presentation. No doubt it will be agreed that the so-called short takes are very much a feature of warm, summer conditions and are not known positively to occur earlier in the season. It is true that there are often touches and nudges in the spring that come to nothing, but these could be caused by trout and parr, and it is generally accepted that the salmon is then in no hurry to part with the lure providing it is not alarmed by feeling resistance through the leader. The short take, therefore, cannot be considered to be a deficiency, either on the part of the angler or the fish, and should be accepted as quite a normal phase of the behaviour of the smaller fish in high summer.

X. Hooking the salmon
Throughout the spring most anglers believe in giving the salmon plenty of time to return to its lie with the lure before

attempting to set the hook. The same drill as suggested for orthodox sunk-line fishing is very reliable with the floating line and is, if anything, easier to perform successfully owing to the better warning of the offer given by the line being visible on the surface. The lowering of the rod point from a suitably high angle and the release of a yard or so of slack line from the left hand is normally enough to allow the fish all the movement required without feeling undue resistance. But if there is any doubt on account of the water being rather deep, or any known tendency in the particular pool for the fish to take near to the side and then return towards the middle, there is no reason why the amount of slack should not be increased by another yard or two if that is preferred. And to repeat, when the weight of the fish eventually begins to be felt, the rod should be bent firmly against it.

When the true summer conditions get established and the river is at normal level or tending low, some modification in the method becomes advisable. In water of moderate depth, it is usually the most suitable to lower the rod as before, but release no slack; while in rather shallow streams it is enough simply to hold the rod still – maintaining the fairly high angle – and wait for the line to tighten against it. Even this latter technique does, of course, give the fish three or four seconds before the line begins to tighten on it, and that is enough for it in its lively state to get back to its lie. Just the straightening of the curve in the line from the rod tip amounts to two or three yards of free movement for the fish, and since its change of position after seizing the fly is rarely directly away from the angler, there is virtually no risk of the strain being felt prematurely.

Once the stage has been reached when it is the best policy to fish much more squarely for the small summer salmon and grilse, however, a decided change in the hooking procedure is necessary. In the first place, the fish are inclined to spit out the fly very quickly; also the drag of the line at its squarish angle across the flow causes the strain to be felt much more quickly by the fish. Therefore it is necessary to tighten smoothly but firmly as soon as the offer has been detected. If this is not done, complaints about short takes will be inevitable.

XI. Appreciation of floating line fishing

Most anglers eventually come round to the view that the take is the most exciting part of salmon fishing. And no-one will dispute that the floating line makes the absolute most of the offers that come, especially when the rise of the salmon is seen on or near the surface. Also there is unquestionably a great deal of extra satisfaction in having induced the salmon to undertake the obviously deliberate rise to meet the subsurface fly.

Seasoned anglers couple with these special pleasures the claim that the floating line is also the easiest form of salmon fishing, both in principle and in practice. Certainly much more of the problem is there to be observed directly than when the presentation of the lure is required to be at the lower levels of the water. And on a good day when the fish are responding well, there is little doubt that a suitable degree of skill with the floating line achieves success more easily and pleasantly than with any other method.

Yet the novice seems to be drawn to the idea that the spinning lure represents his best chance of securing the sport for which he is understandably so impatient. He should, of course, be encouraged to spin when that offers the best promise, but this advice should not be allowed to convey any impression that fly fishing is too difficult for the beginner. And the sooner he can be convinced that the subsurface fly will offer him the most frequent and widespread opportunities of sport, the better it will be.

At the same time, an oversimplified approach to the problems is quite out of place. The details requiring to be considered are surely just the sort of points likely to be of absorbing interest to the enthusiastic new salmon-fisher.

5 Light Spinning

I. Strategy

As the complementary method to the floating line, light spinning is the most versatile method of fishing for salmon and gives almost unlimited scope for the individual to exercise his ingenuity. Great skill is undoubtedly required to make the most of the wide range of opportunities, but possibly more in the form of river-craft than in the handling of the tackle.

The circumstances favouring spinning can be divided into four principal categories:

(a) When the river is higher or carrying more colour than is thought suitable for the subsurface fly.

(b) In clear-water conditions when the weather is too wild for fly fishing.

(c) For covering lies that are inaccessible with fly-fishing tackle owing to overhanging trees or very difficult wading.

(d) For fishing at longer range than is possible with the fly.

During the spring onwards there is the same need as in fly fishing to avoid distracting the salmon by the appearance of the angler within easy view of the lies. The element of surprise is undoubtedly of great importance in the spontaneous response of the salmon to the sudden arrival of the well-presented spinning lure at a time when the peace of the fish is otherwise undisturbed.

Usually only the first two or three casts to cover a particular lie have any chance of success. After a few mintues rest for the fish, it may be worth another attempt, but it can only do harm to let the salmon see the lure repeatedly after it has once been refused.

II. Lures
The range of baits which may be required is very extensive. Devon minnows from about 2½in. to 1½in. in wood, plastic and brass, and lead heavyweights of about 1in.; wobbling spoons; revolving-spoon baits; plugs, and weighted quill-minnows may all be useful.

In much of the downstream fishing, anti-kink leads are just as necessary as in heavy spinning, but chiefly, of course, for the purpose of controlling the speed of the bait. With upstream spinning, however, it is preferable to have all the weight in the bait, although this sometimes means that the rod must be held at a low angle in order to prevent the head-up attitude and too much lift in the bait.

III. Rods, reels and lines
Care must be taken in selecting the rod if a single one is to serve well for all purposes. It must be very easy and comfortable for single-handed use – when necessary it can be steadied by the left hand on the button – but at the one extreme it must be capable of handling weights up to about ¾ oz, and at the other it must be suitable for throwing the lightest baits good distances accurately.

Weight is seldom any problem with modern rods and an eight-footer which will cope well with the heavier work should not be too cumbersome or heavy for the lighter duties. The tip requires to have sufficient power to control the larger baits and, therefore, in order to cast the light baits well, a suitable amount of action in the middle of the rod is necessary.

Some expert casters use small, free-spool multipliers, and do so beautifully. The majority of anglers, however, find the fixed-spool reel to be both efficient and the most easy to use, particularly when casting from a very confined space.

Monofilament is used almost exclusively. One spool loaded with 10–11 lb test will handle all the heavy work, and 7–8 lb test is required on a second spool for casting the lighter baits. It is most important, though, to select a brand which has a very good resistance to stretch. When fishing a very long line, it is almost impossible to secure a firm hook-hold with monofilament that is subject to a lot of elasticity.

Provided a ball-bearing swivel is used between the line and the trace, the fixed-spool reel should give no trouble with kink in the monofilament during the fishing of the bait. When the slipping clutch comes into operation frequently while playing a fish, however, a great deal of kink is invariably put into the line. This will cause no difficulty so long as the line is kept tight at all points from the spool to the fish. But when pumping, one must take care not to lower the rod tip faster than the line is retrieved, otherwise kink may appear in the line between the rod rings and cause a stoppage. And, of course, when the rod is raised in the other half of the pumping action, the forefinger should be placed on the spool to ensure that the slipping clutch does not operate instead of the pressure being exerted on the fish.

When the fish has been landed, the line should be cut above the swivel and a length of fifty or sixty yards run out across the grass and then reeled slowly back onto the spool again. This should remove all the kink and ensure trouble-free casting.

Most modern fixed-spool reels incorporate a trigger-operated optional anti-reverse mechanism, or freedom to wind the reel either way. It keeps kink to the minimum if the slipping clutch is set at a strong pressure and fish are played by turning the reel the reverse way as much as possible to give line when it is necessary.

(Should there be any doubt about the way kink is caused by the slipping clutch, the reason is that winding line onto the spool through the pick-up with the spiralling action automatically puts twist into the line; but when the bait is thrown – or the reel is wound in the reverse direction – the reverse spiralling of the line removes the twist again. But when the slipping clutch is in operation, line is fed through the stationary pick-up from the turning spool, which eliminates the spiralling action and causes the line to retain the twist it had when on the spool. When playing a fish, the repeated recovery of line creating additional twist, and the giving of line by means of the slipping clutch that does nothing to reduce the twist, can easily mean that by the time the fish has been landed, there will be twenty or thirty times as much twist in the line as one single winding onto the reel would create.)

IV. Tactics

During the transitional period and the early part of the true floating-line season, most of the light spinning will be downstream and across in the same way as with the heavy tackle – indeed, there is considerable overlapping, but that is all to the good.

Some modification in the arc fished becomes necessary, however, as the water temperature rises and the fish become more alert. Fig. 12 shows the fishing arc, Y to Z, that would probably be used at about 44°F while W to X would be the kind of change that would be favoured at five or six degrees higher, but in water conditions otherwise the same. It will be seen that the bait, having been thrown much more squarely, travels considerably more with the current for much of its course. And in so doing, it covers the lies at a greater speed.

It may also be necessary for the lure to be rather smaller and fished a little higher in the water. But for this type of

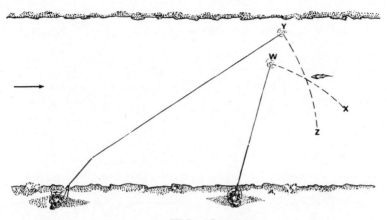

FIG. 12

presentation generally, it remains necessary to use a lead, even if it is quite small. It is best, therefore, to have a relatively light bait so that a fair proportion of the total weight can be in the lead. With the rod held at a high angle, the lead makes it possible to keep a good length of line in the air without it sagging too much, and to control the bait, ensuring that it heads into the flow throughout the arc fished. Without the lead, the line pulls the head of the bait across the current: this pushes it downstream and round very quickly without any possibility of controlling it as desired.

Gradually as the water temperature increases further, however, the rather regimented fishing through an arc along with and across the current begins to lose its appeal to the fish; no doubt because they are able to watch the lure for too long a spell, which thus reduces the element of surprise. At temperatures in the lower fifties, it often becomes necessary to let the salmon have a good·view of the bait only during a rather quick turn. The popular manoeuvre is to stand a few yards upstream of the lie, and cast a good distance further upstream and a little way further across the current (see Fig. 13). Then the bait is retrieved fast enough to outpace the

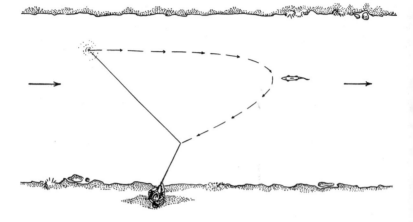

FIG. 13

flow considerably. By the time the lure is opposite the rod, it should be travelling quite quickly and in a line towards the far side of the lie. The speed of retrieve is then regulated so that the bait does a U-turn a couple of yards or so ahead of the fish and about two feet from the bottom. Wood or plastic Devons weighted in the nose are excellent for this purpose, but there is no reason why the wobbling spoon should not be used in the same way when there is some colour in the water and it is thought that more impact may be required.

In this manoeuvre, considerably more variation in the use of the rod is required than in the spinning done previously in the season. While the bait is being drawn quickly downstream, the rod is held high so that a minimum of line is on the water, but as it approaches a position opposite the angler, the rod is lowered to reduce the vertical angle of pull. More line then tends to be submerged and if the current is rather fast, the drag on the line can be enough to swing the bait round with very little further winding of the reel until the lower end of the U-turn has been reached. From that point, a

Above top: Association water on the Spey at Grantown.

Above: The Spey at Tulchan. Some of the finest salmon fishing in the world.

Above top: The Aberdeenshire Dee upstream of Ballater in enchanting scenery.

Above: The Lune at Rigmaden.

steady retrieve brings the bait away in a manner that often seems to be very attractive to the fish, although most of the offers come before that stage.

Also, of course, there is always a chance that a fish will take while the bait is travelling rapidly downstream. Indeed, in a low clear water, even with the surface well ruffled by wind, the U-turn may allow the fish too long a sighting of the lure. Then it becomes necessary to cast upstream from below the lie and guide the bait over the fish rather higher in the water and without checking the speed. When the fish are lively enough to respond to this type of presentation, sport can be possible from steep, heavily treed banks where there are lies that cannot be covered effectively in any other way. Brass Devons are very useful for this class of fishing: in the smaller sizes which may be required, they have enough weight for casting, and the speed at which they are retrieved ensures that they move through the water with a correct posture.

The small, heavyweight Devon is not commonly used, but the few specialists do extremely well with it. In long, fast stretches with many big boulders and deep little pots where the wading is too difficult to cover the water progressively and fully with the fly, odd safe stands can be found here and there. From these, the tiny bait can be cast great distances upstream and retrieved rapidly. From one point or another, the angler can thus cover all the lies. And in this class of spinning, no doubt due to the smallness of the lure and the speed at which it is fished, repeated casts may be made from the same position for some little time before a fish is eventually hooked. Some anglers believe that the salmon requires to see the bait several times before it will take. But it will be appreciated that in that type of current, it could be possible to make numerous apparently similar casts that would result in the bait taking a slightly different course each time. And the high speed of the small lure probably means that it requires to be seen at fairly close quarters to be taken, or to put the fish off.

The particularly appealing feature of this type of fishing, and of fishing from the very difficult, heavily wooded banks, is that anglers who go to such an amount of effort usually fish what is, in effect, virgin water. On the same day, the good, easily-fished pools are probably subjected to too much disturbance. The master of river-craft is certainly not unaware of this.

Another rarely seen use of light spinning is in deep pools that are too steady to be interesting for the floating line, although certain spots may hold fish quite regularly. Periodically a salmon will move round a small circuit, make a swirl on the surface at one point, and then return to the lie. The angler casts from a good distance downstream, drops a light Devon of about 1½in. two or three yards above the lie, and starts retrieving rapidly as soon as the bait touches the water. He may make two or three casts in fairly quick succession, but if there is then no response, he will wait for several minutes before trying again. When an offer comes, it is usually only a second or so after the lure has touched down. Naturally this kind of stalking can be succesful in all sorts of lies, but again it is essential that the fish should have been completely undisturbed before the attempt is made. That is why the enthusiast concentrates on places which are unlikely to attract other anglers.

The main use of light spinning is, of course, when the river is beginning to clear after a spate. The wobbling spoon or plug will take running fish in suitable places, but the most commonly practised method is downstream and across with Devons as in the earlier days of the season. And although large numbers of salmon are undoubtedly caught in this way, the noticeably uneven spread of the catches among the rods shows that the individual's river-craft is a crucial factor even in these relatively easy conditions for catching salmon.

One rather common mistake is to concentrate too much on fishing close to the bottom in the deeper water, probably while wading in the areas that would be more likely to yield fish if approached suitably. This rather extensive question, however, will be dealt with in the next chapter.

6 Salmon Lies and Resting Places

The manual skills in fishing for salmon are much more readily learnt than the ability to judge, according to the time of the year and the ruling conditions, the type of lie that will probably be favoured by fish that may be in the taking mood.

In order to get a sound grasp of this problem, numerous factors concerning both the disposition of the fish and the character of the flow near the bed of the river must be considered in detail. Naturally, each one of these is quite easy to understand. The difficulty lies in the fact that much of the required information is not directly observable. The indirect guides, however, are very reliable and when interpreted reasonably well, they will serve the angler quite satisfactorily even on unfamiliar water.

I. Runs and glides
First it is necessary to visualize the essential differences between the two basic types of flow. Runs through the necks of pools and narrow sections, and the streamy water in the wider, more shallow stretches, have a rough or popply surface. This is a good indication that the inherent forward impetus in the water — created by the effects of gravity in the area of the decline in the bed of the river higher

upstream – is very irregular in its strength. One ribbon of faster flow gains on another that is a little slower, and there are movements and divisions between them in all planes – forward, downward, upward and sideways. At the lower levels of the water, irregularities in the bottom cause a great deal of turbulence – once again, in all directions. And in the aggregate, there is a much greater net movement of water downstream in the upper layers than the lower ones. Also, proportionate to the force of the flow, the shallower the water, the rougher is the turbulence near the bottom; while in deep water, a boisterous surface current may well leave the lower levels quite placid. Thus a run of varying depth is often quite capable of providing lies to suit the needs of the salmon at any period of the season.

A popply current, in either a shallow stream or a deepish run, is also most helpful to the angler from the physical point of view. Both the sunk line and the floater tend to lodge in the steadier areas between the ribbons of faster flow; and although the overall force eventually pushes the line to the side, it does so in a conveniently manageable way. And to a lesser degree, the spinning line is assisted in a like manner. Hence the type of flow that is the most generally suitable to be tenanted by interested salmon is also favourable for presenting the lure successfully.

Glides behave entirely differently. The water itself is quite inert and moves along en masse owing to the pull of the suction created immediately below, where a drop in the bed of the river enables gravity to take hold forcefully. As the smooth surface of the glide indicates, there is a minimum of turbulence at all levels; hence the flow is very nearly even throughout the depth of the water. But the smoothness can be very deceptive in respect of the speed of the glide. The flow in a narrow, shallowing glide at the tail of a big, deep, still-looking pool, is often much faster than the most rapid of the runs and streams.

In normal circumstances during most of the season, salmon

do not lie in glides. The smooth, even flow gives them no help to hold their positions without too much expenditure of effort and energy. Also, the speed is often faster than suits their rate of respiration. And the same features that cause glides to be difficult for the salmon make them extremely unhelpful to the angler in his efforts to control the line and present the lure correctly. A free body that is heavier than water drops to the bottom through gliding water more directly and quickly than in areas of variable flow and turbulence. But the line, being restrained by the rod, is pushed upward and to the side by what amounts to a solid wall of water on the move. On the few occasions — such as in very hot weather — when it may be worth fishing a strong glide at normal level, the only means of attaining suitable control over the lure is by sheer weight. The fly must be very heavy relative to its bulk, or the spinner should be aided by a substantial lead.

Any rise in the level of the river naturally causes changes, which although very noticeable, are often even more far reaching than is apparent. Indeed, almost complete reversals can take place between the relative values of runs and glides.

II. Spates

The big runs of salmon usually take place while the river is returning to normal level following a spate. In the early months there may be a comparatively small amount of colour and suspended matter in the water while the level is still very high. Soon after the crest has moved down into the estuary, the salmon may start moving into the lower pools of the river and with a minimum of delay they will occupy the main lies in the deep water.

Later in the season after the river systems have been at low levels, exposing silt and sand banks to dry out in the sunshine, and allowing the accumulation of all sorts of natural deposits between the low and high water marks, spates can be very dirty and rather foul. The extra water is liable to carry a far greater amount of solid matter in suspension, particularly at the lower levels of the lies in the runs that suit the salmon so well when the river is in generally good form.

The fish may start to run as soon as the crest of the spate has passed below them. By then, however, the upper layers of the water in which they travel will be comparatively free from colour and objectionable matter, but the lower levels in the deeper water may still be quite foul. Consequently the main lies for the fish in normal circumstances would be quite untenantable; although at this juncture the fact is rather irrelevant, because the needs of the fish are now different and are better suited by the resting places and high-water lies.

III. Resting places

The good pace of the surface layers of water when the river is above normal level satisfies the needs of the salmon for running extremely well. The speed of the flow matches their requirements in respect of the rate of respiration, and the lateral variations in the pace of the current enables them to maintain speedy and almost effortless progress upstream. The shape of the body and its correct positioning between different strengths of flow enable the fish to utilize the more powerful current to help in propelling itself forward alongside a slightly weaker force of water. An occasional flick of the tail seems to be all that is necessary to keep the salmon moving forward at a remarkably good pace.

When taking a short rest, the salmon obviously favours the same speed of flow for its respiratory requirements as when on the move. And naturally when the track that it is following leads the fish to a point where the water is suitably shallow for it simply to halt and take a rest close to the bottom, it is far more convenient than if it were to have to make a diversion and seek out a suitable spot for a breather. A foot or so of water is plenty deep enough, while more than about three feet would probably have little appeal for this purpose.

In this context, there are two features of glides during a spate that make them very attractive as resting places. One that is confined within high, rocky banks and simply becomes deeper and faster, of course, remains uninteresting But in the many cases where the water can spread laterally and find new outlets into the rapid below, the single glide, in effect; becomes a series of connected glides of varying strengths lying side by side. The slight swirls on the surface of the water indicate the areas which are subject to suctional pulls from different directions. Such spots often make ideal resting places. And the other helpful factor is that since the speed of the water is practically the same near the bottom as it is on the surface, the salmon show no objection to moving along the bottom into rather deeper water until they find the exact pace of flow they require for resting. Hence at this stage there is a complete reversal of the normal position regarding the potential value to the angler of the runs and the glides.

It is by no means a matter of chance that the availability of good resting places also suits the salmon in respect of the way in which they are located. Short spells of rest are naturally most wanted before and after negotiating difficult stretches. A rapid containing much white water and perhaps requiring the fish to make a leap here and there usually terminates upstream in a favourable glide, while at the downstream end where the river is wider there will probably be some reasonably fast and shallow water close to the bank which will offer the right kind of accommodation.

Resting places in glides are often doubly valuable, however, because of difficult water both above and below. Smooth, deep pools with very little flow when the river is at normal height take on much of the character of an unbroken glide when a spate comes. The evenness of the flow for most of the breadth of the river gives the fish no assistance in travelling; and if it extends for more than a short distance, the tracks chosen by the salmon are likely to be close to the sides where there may be some turbulance and variation in the flow caused by boulders or irregularities in the banks. Even so, that class of water represents very hard work compared with places where there is a nice, lively stream in the surface layer. Hence a shallowing, disrupted glide situated between a long, smooth pool and the broken water of a heavy rapid, has an outstandingly good potential as a regularly attractive place for running fish to rest.

The reverse, however, applies in the case of the type of gliding water best suited for catching salmon while they are actually travelling. There require to be good resting places both above and below, thus encouraging the salmon to undertake the relatively hard work of moving directly ahead through the smooth flow and not to seek an easier course along the edge of the river. This assumes, of course, that the salmon have an instinctive appreciation of what lies ahead for some distance up the river, but their behaviour in respect of the regular tracks they follow directly through some glides and skirting others leaves no doubt of their awareness of the nature of the flow towards which they are moving.

IV. High-water lies

When eventually a salmon reaches the pool in which it is going to settle for some time, the river may still be too high for the main lies in the runs to be sufficiently free from suspended matter. And in any case, after the early months of the year, the fish will probably show a preference following a spell of running for a fairly shallow and fast lie for several hours providing it does not get disturbed. Nevertheless, the most favoured places are usually alongside the deeper spots that will become attractive as the level of the river falls.

Gradually deepening water covering a bed of gravel on the inside of a big, wide bend in the river is particularly good in this respect. Slight lateral movements by the fish offer them the nicely graduated changes they may wish concerning both the speed of the flow and the depth. Such places are also among the first to be free from the suspended matter which the fish dislike so much.

V. Permanency of lies

In rock-bound pools that are reasonably free from accumulations of silt, sand and fine gravel, all the resting places and lies — both high water and normal — may remain completely unchanged for many years. Needless to say, precise knowledge of such spots for different heights of the water is invaluable. Particularly in the case of resting places in glides, it is often necessary to drop the lure in one exact position relative to that of the fish if it is to take. Details of this sort are naturally just as important as knowing the location of the lie.

On stretches where there are large gravel beds that are subject to shifting, almost imperceptible changes in the lies take place after every spate and one must be careful not to put too much reliance on one particular cast being the crucial test of whether the resident in the lie is interested. Big floods in the valley, however, can cause a complete redistribution of the gravel beds, the destruction of all the old lies, and the establishment of entirely new ones. But so long as the main channel always remains within the same high-water limits despite the water spilling over and covering low-lying land, it is remarkable how often the apparently new location of the river bed and changed positions of the gravel banks seem to be an almost exact repeat of the situation that existed during a previous period, possibly many years earlier. The explanation for this can be seen if the high-water marks of the unusually big floods are recorded. The run-offs from the fields as the flood recedes come into play differently according to the height reached by the water, and it is the effects of these variations on the dispositions of the gravel beds that create the tendency for previously-seen patterns to be re-established.

Big floods on all stretches should be seen as a warning both to make a check of all the familiar lies and to investigate thoroughly the possibility that valuable new lies will have come into existance.

VI. Fishing spates

Anglers become so accustomed to ignoring, or wading through shallow water beside the main current when the water is at normal height, that there is a common tendency grossly to underestimate the potential as resting places of many of the little areas close to the bank that would be very easy to cover correctly with fly or spinner. The more impossible it may look on a particular stretch when the fish are running in a big water that there could be any good places for the angler to fish, the more probable it is that any spot known to be shallow will be holding a resting fish. Although the current may appear to be altogether too fast, every such place should be given a serious trial. On some occasions after having caught a salmon, it still seems incredible that one would be resting in such fast water. And once any position has produced an offer from a fish, it can be expected that it will be tenanted again repeatedly during the current and future spates. Indeed, one resting place is often well capable of producing several salmon in the day.

As the water drops back, there should be no great hurry to start fishing the main lies. The high-water lies are much the easier to fish correctly and promise the best as long as they remain occupied.

In summer, small salmon and grilse frequently keep on with a kind of running after the water has dropped back to normal level and has become quite clear. A shoal may remain in one pool for a couple of hours or so and then, still as a group, the fish will move steadily up some streamy water and into the next holding pool. Their movements are very much like the low-geared variety of running sometimes adopted by the autumn-run salmon. Having stayed in one lie for a spell, a fish will move unhurriedly along the bottom to the next lie, and so on. And in such a case, the grilse and small salmon are practically certain to be in a good taking mood the whole of the time. Frequently the fish show on the surface so much that it is possible for the angler to move up the river pool by pool and maintain productive contact with them throughout the beat.

On other occasions, the small fish behave in a very similar manner, but as individuals, or in small parties of two or three. Then the best policy is to concentrate either on the spots where they tend to linger the longest, or on the places where they seem least able to resist taking the small fly. A good stream of about three or four feet in depth often attracts an interesting accumulation of fish and in such a case, it will probably stand being fished down numerous times providing it is rested for fifteen minutes or so between operations. But long, shallow glides that gradually taper away to ankle-deep water frequently produce offers the most readily. It is quite common to see the back and dorsal fin show above the smooth surface of the glide as the small fish makes its faltering way upstream. Then it is usually not difficult to lead the fly round in front of the grilse with an excellent chance that it will be taken with a beautiful little head-and-tail rise.

VII. Choice of method at spate time
The majority of anglers seem to have more confidence in spinning than in fly fishing when the river is carrying extra water. The spinning lure, especially when aided by a lead, is undoubtedly the most suitable for fishing slowly in glides and strong currents. But in the more shallow and steady of the high-water lies and resting places, it is the fly that can be fished the more slowly and at a controlled, suitable depth.

On stretches where the pressure of rods limits one's scope, the less popular spots may well be very suitable for the fly and would probably offer better prospects of sport than the potentially better casts that tend to be continuously over-fished.

7 Scope for Developments

Ingenious anglers over the years have probably tried every conceivable variation in fishing for salmon and it is unlikely that any basically new method could be devised. Indeed, the *new tactics* that one hears about from time to time are almost invariably rediscoveries of very old ideas that have not won continuous, widespread popularity. Nevertheless, there is undoubtedly plenty of scope left for refinements, particularly in respect of the application of old concepts in ways which are singularly well suited to the disposition of the fish in the more unhelpful circumstances.

The time of the year when the angler is most likely to feel the need for a better way to tackle some of the difficulties is, of course, in summer when the problem of deceiving the salmon is a much more delicate matter than when the temperature of the water is lower. The success of the established lures in the less trying of the summer conditions suggests that there is more room for improvements in the details of presentation than in the design of flies and spinners. And it would seem that the two factors that have been the least fully exploited, and therefore offer the most interesting possibilities, are the element of surprise and unusual approaches by the lure into the taking zone of the fish.

I. Escape tactics

The idea is to make the lure rise up through the water as it approaches and covers the lie of the salmon. This can be done almost equally well with spinners, sunk flies and small flies. It is, of course, an adaptation of the old *sink and draw* method, simulating the action of a small fish when attempting to escape from danger near the bed of the river.

With the spinner, or the large fly on the sunk line, the lure is fished as close to the bottom as possible until it reaches a point two or three yards upstream of the fish and a yard or so further across the current. The rod is then raised gently from a low angle and at the same time, a little line is retrieved slowly, either by reeling or drawing with the left hand as the case may be. This pressure combined with the force of the current will bring the lure sweeping up to the surface, but also still moving downstream slightly. The movement of the lure should be continued until it does, in fact, break surface, because some of the offers do not come until the very last moment.

The drill with the floating line is to cast to the point from which a big upstream mend will align the leader and several yards of the line with the flow and place the fly five or six yards upstream of the lie. Then the rod point is lowered and everything is allowed to drift with the current as fast as possible. This allows the fly to sink quickly and when the line begins to tighten, the rod is raised gently so that the line is checked quite hard. Again, the lure rises to the surface in front of the salmon.

This manoeuvre will often succeed when a fish has been seen to perform two or three head-and-tail rises from its lie, but has not responded to the lure presented in the orthodox manner. One assumes that at least on some occasions it is the rather novel movement of the lure, in its own right, that brings the reaction of the fish. But there is perhaps more likelihood that it is the combination of the faster speed of the lure resulting in a more deceptive illusion and the fact that this is achieved without the lure moving away beyond taking range. Also, in many cases, the element of surprise may be involved to an appreciable extent. In many states of the light, the image of the lure at the low angle of sight before it starts to lift through the water may make only a negligible impact on the fish, but as the angle of sight increases and the background changes, so may the impact of the lure progressively become greater.

It is a very convenient manoeuvre since it can be tried at almost any time without having to make any special preparations.

II. The extended dangle

When the river is low, particularly in warm weather, the salmon often tend to congregate in narrow guts where the speed of the current is extraordinarily fast. In many such places it is possible to take up a position from which the lure can be held at the dangle in the middle of the flow or thereabouts. With the light spinning outfit, a small Devon is dropped into the current with the bale arm of the reel left in the casting position, and the line checked by the forefinger against the lip of the spool. Then the line is released a yard or two at a time and checked again momentarily between each forward movement of the bait so that it fishes its way jerkily but quite rapidly downstream. Only the first two or three appearances of the lure are likely to bring any response, but after reasonable periods of rest the suitable spots can be tried several times in the day, each with the chance that the lure will take a different and possibly more effective line of travel.

A similar action can be achieved with a fairly heavy tube-fly, or a bulkily-dressed conventional fly, on either the sunk or the floating line, but the drill by which the loops of line are released successively by the left hand has to be worked out carefully. With the floating line, a tube-fly of about 1½in. can be made to bobble about rather crazily on the surface, dipping down here and there, and this can be very effective on occasions.

Seemingly in the very rough and fast water, the spinner or fly comes into view of the fish very suddenly and must be taken almost immediately if the opportunity is not to be lost altogether. Thus the element of surprise is perhaps exploited to its maximum potential.

The big tube-fly bobbling near the surface has been cited from time to time as an example in the attempt to refute the water temperature/size concept as far as it concerns subsurface flies. It will be appreciated, however, that the suggestion is quite irrelevant. The orthodox, subsurface fly requires to maintain a suitable illusion after having been in range of detailed scrutiny for a comparatively great length of time, while in this context the big tube-fly, to be effective, must seem to appear suddenly from nowhere and make an instant impact. There is no more relationship between the two situations than there is between the fast-moving spinner and the subsurface fly. And clearly, when the element of surprise is the crucial factor, the limitations in respect of the size of the lure are not nearly so narrow.

No doubt the mention of the extended dangle will prompt the thought that it is much the same as upstream spinning, but there is a considerable difference. In the very fast water that is suitable for this manoeuvre – with which the lure travels at the speed of the flow or slower – the bait cast upstream would have to be retrieved a deal faster than the flow if it were to perform as a spinner is required to do; and then it would probably pass over the fish much too quickly for an interception to be possible. Also there is the question of access. Suitably fast water of this type often terminates in a big, deep, slack pool where it would be impossible – excepting from a boat – to get into the position from which the lies could be covered from the downstream end.

III. The dry fly for salmon
Salmon have certainly been caught on the dry fly in Britain,

but as yet the technique cannot be said to have really emerged from the experimental stage. This is probably partly because the American experts have not made their trials here in the most suitable circumstances, with the result that there has been no impressively favourable publicity to encourage widespread, practical interest in the method. But perhaps the main reason is the vagueness of the information that has been generally available.

From detailed enquiries and a certain amount of first-hand experience, it seems that there are a few essential, basic requirements for the dry fly to offer reasonably serious prospects of sport. Firstly, the water temperature must be rather high, 60°F probably being about the minimum; and secondly there should be a good, healthy flow with the surface fairly smooth or slightly rippled, but not rough. Naturally, these requirements of a good height of relatively warm water tend to limit the time when the suitable conditions are likely to apply to the summer period. Hence it would seem that only the small summer salmon and grilse – in the class of fresh-run fish – are very promising subjects for trials with the dry fly.

Regarding the flies, the general impression seems to be that they should be rather big and bushy, but it can be said definitely that on some occasions, such dressings failed completely when others that were very little bigger than an ordinary dry-fly for trout succeeded in taking small salmon and grilse.

One effective drill is to watch for a fish to show on the surface a couple of times in the same place and then, from a position opposite to, or slightly downstream from the lie, to drop the fly a yard or two above the fish and let it drift down as free from serious drag as possible. The small floater may then be taken with the minimum of disturbance – just the neb of the fish protruding inobtrusively above the surface – and the line should be tightened firmly with practically no delay, but not hurriedly. If the fish feels the pull of the leader before the hook has been set, it will almost certainly succeed in getting rid of the fly.

The advantage of the dry-fly — when the fish are willing to take it — is no doubt due to the fact that a more illusory image is seen when the lure has to be viewed through the surface film of the water. The details of colour, or tone, and form cannot be seen with the same precision as in the case of the subsurface fly, especially during the approach to the taking zone.

Probably on some occasions when the small salmon and grilse are responding well to the subsurface fly, the dry-fly would also be effective. But the dry fly would be valued more highly if it could be established reasonably widely that it is capable of taking fish during some of the times when the subsurface lure is being consistently refused. In that context, the month of August comes to mind.

Another North American idea that sometimes does well with the grilse is to put a half-hitch in the leader round the shank of the hook about a quarter of an inch down from the eye. This tends to make the lure skate rather jerkily on the surface, which is loosely classed by some anglers as dry-fly fishing. It is at its most effective when used in a medium-rough current and some of the takes are very exciting slashes at the fly. Here again, there should be no undue delay in setting the hook.

8 Circumstantial Evidence

The life cycle of the salmon must be one of the most adventurous, demanding and hazardous that has to be endured by any living creature. Hence its survival as a species – quite apart from the added complications of the harm done by man – must surely be seen to refute suggestions that the behavioural scheme imposed on the fish by nature is in any way irrational, suicidal, or subject to optional, whimsical activities which are opposed to the principle of self preservation.

It is often purported to be an aberration that when in one of its exuberant moods, the salmon will respond to the angler's lure, although it does not feed in fresh water. But this aspect of the behaviour of the fish – for which we ought to be ever thankful – is in all other respects entirely harmless and free from any risk. And clearly, the test of the rationality of nature is not that a species should be invulnerable to the devices of man.

The evidence of the crucial factor of the taking mood and the associated problems, of course, must be classed as circumstantial, thus excluding the possibility of reaching factual conclusions. And there is no authority able to adjudicate any opinion to be the right one. The individual has no option other than to make his own decisions concerning the views that are acceptable and those that should be rejected. The resulting opinion is purely a personal one, and must be his own responsibility.

With this in mind, I resisted the temptation to relate fishing experiences of my own in the text, hoping that the reader would not be distracted in any way from associating the abstract narrative with the stretches of rivers he knows, with his personal observations of the salmon, and with his own successes with the rod.

I believe that every point made will be endorsed by one angler or another. In the case of a reader who is familiar with salmon fishing at all times throughout the season, there is the possibility that this book will prove simply to be a record of his own opinions and beliefs — perhaps long-held. Should this be so, it may be some satisfaction to him to know that another angler is in full agreement.

9 Choice of River

Before the appearance of UDN, the trend of the cyclic changes affecting the various classes of salmon seemed to be that grilse and small summer fish were becoming more numerous, and to a lesser extent, the autumn runs were improving. There were fears, though, that the spring runs were on the decline, but the position in this respect may have been distorted by the then growing amount of netting at sea.

Since then the damage done by the disease appears to have been proportionately the most serious among the springers. And the nett result of all the influences — both the natural events and the interference by man — is that summer fishing offering satisfactory prospects of sport is by far the most plentiful and reliable, while the autumn salmon are doing remarkably well in the circumstances.

It is expected that UDN, and hoped that sea netting, will both prove to be relatively short-term factors; and eventually the new state of the healthy and less-violated stocks of salmon will be manifested. In the meantime, however, it is already clear that the standards of the past two or three decades regarding the relative merits of the various classes of river and the different periods of the salmon season will no longer hold good. And although a factual reappraisal cannot yet be made, it is certainly not too soon for the individual to be envisaging the changes which might be needed in the planning of fishing trips for the not too distant future.

Since personal taste is so important in this respect, it may be necessary to give some thought to the principal features of unfamiliar types of rivers and thus perhaps minimize the risk of disappointment with a new venue.

Spate streams should be considered first, because they give a useful, scaled-down view of the performance of many of the larger rain-fed rivers. The proportion of the rainfall that is able to penetrate the surface and be held back long enough to feed the stream after the spate has passed is insufficient to provide a suitable flow for normal, day to day salmon fishing. But sport while the summer spate is subsiding is usually hectic – hence the name given to these famous little rivers.

Many anglers prefer the more regular routine of fishing bigger rivers, but devotees of the spate streams claim that they offer thrills that are unknown elsewhere, while the little river in its pomp, with plentiful evidence of lively salmon and sea trout, is an incomparable sight. The excitement begins as soon as the first heavy drops of the coming downpour hit the ground and it is then known that if the rain continues for just a few hours, the stream will be completely transformed. The first effect of the rain on the salmon-fishing beats is a pre-spate rise of almost clear water, probably with a lot of leaves floating on the surface. The increased flow arouses the salmon that are already resident in the pools and they become practically certain takers during the short spell before the colour arrives and the water wells up rapidly. Then there is no chance of sport while the level continues to rise, but as soon as the crest of the spate has passed and the surface becomes free from floating debris, fishing should no longer be delayed. The small subsurface fly does extremely well. Local experts usually say that a Low Water no. 8, or its equivalent, is far more effective than anything larger.

At some stage while the spate is subsiding, depending on the distance of the beat from the estuary, fresh-run fish are likely to arrive in the pools. They tend to show on the surface a great deal and everyone can expect to have sport.

On the smaller spate-streams, the favourable fishing levels may only last for a matter of five or six hours. But this gives rather a unique kind of contentment to some anglers. Being able to cover the small pools with no shortcoming and fish throughout the good period, they can then relax with the thought that they have availed themselves fully of the opportunities; and no irksome doubt concerning the time when one ought to have fished can arise.

There are short taking-times on spate streams when the water is at normal level and clear, and the skilful angler is able to catch the occasional salmon. But with no help from the water in the way of providing concealment and presenting the fly suitably, the difficulties should not be underestimated. At dusk, however, there is often an excellent chance of sport that is well within the capabilties of anyone who can put out a short line. The best spots are where little stretches of fast, shallow water run into deep holes in which the salmon lie during the daytime. When the light begins to go, both salmon and sea trout tend to nose up into the more aerated water. A Low Water no. 6 Blue Charm fishing slowly across the flow and just beneath the surface can be relied upon to be taken boldly by both species when the conditions are right to tempt them into the faster water. A sky free from any very bright patches is the most favourable.

In principle the only difference between the spate streams and the so-called rain-fed rivers is that in the catchments of the latter there is proportionately much less surface drainage with the result that more of the rainfall is delayed underground on the lower slopes of the mountains: thus a reasonably good fishing level is maintained for quite a long period after a spate. In all other respects, a beat on a rain-fed river is simply a magnified version of its counterpart on a spate stream. It takes more rain to produce a comparable increase in the volume of the water, a longer period before the river begins to rise, and so on.

On a major river a good spate will usually leave the water at a particularly favourable level for a week or more; and even in the absence of further rain, many of the pools will continue to fish well almost indefinitely. There are, of course, high-water and low-water stretches – both can be most important and a first class beat should include some of each. Generally, however, the opportunities to fish with a reasonable chance of success are very much less restricted. Nevertheless, these grand waters lack the charm of smaller rivers for some anglers. Huge pools put a premium on good casting. This is no hardship to those who are able to fish frequently, but it can prove rather strenuous for anglers who cannot keep in fairly constant practice. It is understandable if they feel more at ease and confident on the medium sized and smaller rivers, although these are more dependent on frequent spells of wet weather.

The question of the present state of the stocks of salmon is also an important consideration when comparing the pros and cons of the size of a river. One really good run of fish can provide interesting prospects of sport for an appreciably long period on the majority of the good beats on a smallish river. But the same number of salmon spreading up a major river would hardly be noticed on most of the reaches at any one time. Some beats would probably do well for a short period, of course, but a succession of huge runs of any particular class of salmon is necessary to produce the potential that gave the famous big rivers their great reputations.

The large runs of grilse in recent years on some of the major rivers, however, present some attractive possibilities. The spring-fishing beats often remain unlet during the summer months and there would seem to be scope for enterprising anglers who are suitably informed of events in the estuaries, to exploit the opportunities which may arise.

Short rivers that drain large sheets of still water, and the few salmon rivers which are fed mainly by springs in the chalk downs, are notable for the fact that they are not subject to very sudden spates and are maintained at suitable fishing levels for long periods despite dry weather. One of the resultant, chief characteristics is that the best taking places tend to remain the same year after year. This has its obvious advantages, but it can also encourage too stereotyped a view of fishing policy. Most of the loch- and lake-fed rivers also have good runs of grilse and sea trout. The pools can appear to be almost entirely unpopulated one day and the next they may be alive with fish. Hence one's hopes can always remain much higher than when the middle or upper reaches of a long river are understocked and the news from downstream is discouraging.

Hydro schemes are now the dominant factor on some well-known rivers. Local information is essential in such cases. When there are big variations in the flow at different hours of the day, the natural taking times cease to be the main influence on the fish. A sudden increase in the flow of clear water is somewhat similar to the pre-spate rise elsewhere after heavy rain. Usually it will bring the fish on to the take and also encourage fresh runs from the estuary. Some anglers may like to know that at a certain hour, they will almost certainly be able to start catching fish. Others feel more satisfaction in finding their sport where the natural regime is in control of the environment.

Perhaps this glimpse at the problem will serve to show how valuable it can be to read some of the fishing books written by the famous anglers of earlier years who became closely identified with particular rivers. Their references to tackle may be out of date and some of the beliefs they expressed may not now be credible. But often their descriptions of the pools and the character of the rivers in general are so good and thorough as to be little less informative than a personal visit. Much that is said accentuates the sadness of the position today in many areas. However, the great joy of salmon fishing cannot be measured quantitatively. Times are different, but there are surely wonderful days ahead for those who have a genuine appreciation of beautiful rivers and seek out the kind of fishing that pleases them the most.